GROWING UP

BEFORE YOUR CHILDREN DO

Betty
Stewart, M.A.

 THE HAVEN CORPORATION

Published by The Haven Corporation, 802 Madison Avenue, Evanston, Illinois 60202.

First Edition

Library of Congress Cataloging in Publication Data
Stewart, Betty
Growing Up Before Your Children Do
I. Title
82-84243
ISBN: 0-911361-03-0

Printed in the United States of America

A child is a person who is going to carry on what you have started. He is going to sit where you are sitting, and when you are gone, attend to those things which you think are important. You may adopt all the policies you please, but how they are carried out depends on him.

He will assume control of your cities, states, and nations. He is going to move in and take over your churches, schools, universities and corporations . . . the fate of humanity is in his hands.

Abraham Lincoln

CONTENTS

INTRODUCTION

This book is dedicated to and written for all the children and their families whom I've seen in family therapy. They have taught me much about courage and about love and about faith. We have laughed together and cried together and learned from one another. And when they have asked me, "What can I read?" I've said, "One of these days I'm going to write a book about all these things that I think are so important."

One of these days has come, and the book is written. I hope it is helpful to all those who have asked for it, and for those whom I've never met and probably never will. I apologize for its incompleteness—it's impossible to adequately cover everything in one book—and for any impression I may give that I believe being a good parent is easy or even always possible.

After almost thirty years of parenting, I'm keenly aware that we all make mistakes out of inexperience or unresolved unhappiness or because of traumatic events that may temporarily cause us to neglect our children. Luckily for all of us, our children usually forgive us our mistakes and love us anyway. Since most of us become parents long before we are fully grown up and mature ourselves, the job of parenting sometimes is a race against time as we try to grow up before our children do. While we struggle to rid ourselves of inadequacies or fears or anxieties or guilts that we have carried over from our own childhood, we must at the same time try to help our children avoid those same feelings.

To be a good parent therefore becomes a matter of balancing our children's needs against our own, and of being responsible caretakers while we pursue our own dreams and goals. That isn't an easy task, and while it's good to hold an ideal in mind of the kind of parents we want to be, it's also important to realize that we can't be perfect, and to forgive ourselves when we fall short of our ideal.

The ideas in this book are those that I believe are the most important in helping children grow up healthy and well-adjusted. They are also the ideas that I believe should have priority with parents who want to grow up before their children do.

This book isn't intended to teach people how to be *perfect* parents, but to help them be *better* parents. I hope it helps, because I believe every child deserves the best parents he can possibly have.

*You can learn many things from
children. How much patience
you have, for instance.*
                    -Franklin P. Jones

Chapter One

DON'T BE AFRAID,
YOU'RE SMARTER THAN THEY ARE
(AND IT'S YOUR HOUSE!)

Your child is not your enemy. In fact, in most cases, your child will be the best friend you'll ever have. She will love you when you're bad-tempered and unreasonable, she will accept you when you're ugly and sloppy and messy, she will be loyal to you when you are less then perfect, and she will overlook it when you are indiscreet or embarrassing.

Who else will be that devoted to you? Who else will deliver you a fistful of flowers filched from the neighbor's yard and with eyes shining with love, say, "I picked you some flowers, Mommy, 'cause you're so pretty!"

Who else will ceremoniously open the bathroom door while you're sitting on the toilet and with a proud flourish, announce to his friends, "That's my Dad!"

And who else will come and snuggle next to you in the evening when you're dead tired and dejected and lonely and gently pat your cheek and say, "I luvja, Mommy."

You won't get that kind of uncritical love and devotion from anybody else in the world, and you will still have it when your child is an adult with children of his own if you accept your child as completely as he accepts you. That means that you love him when *he's* bad-tempered and unreasonable, and when he's dirty and sloppy and smelly, and when he's not perfect, and when he does things that embarrass you. Truly, in matters of love and loyalty, every adult can learn a lot from the way a child loves, with no strings attached and with no restrictions. Parents are often afraid to simply love and accept a child as he is, for fear that they will be failing in their duty to teach and guide their child in a better direction. To get an idea of how that affects a child, imagine that you are working in your yard, and you notice some rosebuds just about to burst into bloom. You cut them and go into the house where your wife is busy in the kitchen, and with feelings of love and romance, say to her, "Look, honey, here are the first roses of the garden this year."

There are several ways she could react, but the one that would probably make you feel happiest would be for her to take the roses, kiss you warmly, and say, "Thank you! They're lovely. Let's put them on the dining table."

Imagine how crushed you would feel, however, if she said, "My God, you're filthy! How can you stand that dirt under your fingernails? You're going to have to take a bath before dinner!"

Or imagine that you bowl a game you're very proud of, and when you get home you tell your husband, "Hey, I bowled a 280 tonight!"

If he says, "Wow! That's great, you're getting to be a terrific bowler!" you'll feel loved and appreciated and motivated. But if he says, "If you had tried harder, you could have bowled 300," you're not going to feel very happy toward yourself, your husband, or bowling.

The point is that being a good parent doesn't mean being a continual teacher and guide and rule-setter. In fact, it makes absolutely no difference how much you try to motivate, teach, or change your child. She will learn from your example and from the examples of other important people in her life, and not from anything anybody preaches to her. You will both be happier and your family will operate much more smoothly if you relax and enjoy your child and accept the fact that she is not perfect in every respect, and that she never will be, any more than you are or ever will be.

In order to do this, of course, you must first accept the fact of your own imperfection, and accept the fact that it's okay not to be perfect in every way. Parents always hate and fear the same things in their children that they hate and fear in themselves, and if they see behavior in their children that they reject in themselves, they may so self-righteously reject that behavior in the child that they reject the whole child.

If you can only love and accept your daughter when she's clean and dressed in a cute little dress, or if you can't stand for your son to touch you because his hands feel sticky and messy, or if it makes you furious when your child has a temper tantrum or spills a glass of milk at dinner or tracks mud on the dining room floor, you need to learn to accept the objectionable parts of yourself which you are rejecting in your child.

It's not only safe to accept the imperfections in yourself and in your child, but it's also safe to let your child know that you have imperfections. He won't love you any less for them, and may in fact be more cooperative when he knows you're not infallible. For example, if you're cutting a board for a closet shelf and it turns out to be two inches too short and you have to redo it, it's okay to simply say, "I measured it wrong. I'll do it again and get it right this time."

Your child will learn several things which you could never teach in a lecture or deliberate lesson. He will learn that it is possible to make a mistake even with the best of intentions, and that most mistakes can be rectified, even though it takes more time and energy to rectify them.

On the other hand, if you curse your ruler, or snarl at your child to get out of your way, or curse yourself for being a fool, or abandon the entire project, he will learn a different type of lesson, and it will make absolutely no difference what you preach to him about finishing what he begins, or about taking the responsibility for his own actions, or about having self-respect, or about owning up to his own mistakes.

Many times, parents have the idea that being a parent means that when they are with their children they have to behave like a *parent*—whatever that means—and not like themselves. The truth is that there is no special way of behaving like a parent, and you can only be the person you are. To be sure, there are responsibilities that parents have, but you don't have to be a different person when you carry out those responsibilities. You may be a little zany or a little pedantic or a little overly sentimental or a little overly intellectual, and if you are, you'll just have to be a zany parent or a pedantic parent or one who cries at every dance recital or who reads Proust during PTA meetings. If you are wacky and try to curb your wackiness and behave in some stilted stereotyped parental mold, you will only confuse yourself and your child, and you won't be a better parent.

If you grew up watching *Leave it to Beaver* and *My Three Sons* and *Ozzie and Harriet*, you may believe those TV characters were the ideal parents and try to be just like them. That's fine if you really are just like them, but there are a lot of other good parental types in the world, too.

You may be a mother who much prefers exploring some desolate part of the country for dinosaur tracks to staying home cleaning house, you may be a father who would rather bake bread than go hunting, or you may be parents with two careers which are very important to you both. Or you may be a divorced or widowed mother or father trying to juggle your children with a career and a social life. Your success as a parent doesn't depend on what kind of social role or marital role you play, or on how much time you spend with your children, it depends on how you relate to them when you're with them.

If you accept your children as they are, and love them for what they are without demanding idealistic expectations of perfection, and if you allow them to accept you as you are without trying to hide or excuse your imperfections—but always trying to grow up before your children do—you may not only be as good a parent as the stereotyped models, you may even be better than Beaver's parents.

What Obedience Is And Is Not

Very often when I'm talking to parents who are having problems with their children, the parents say something like, "I'm just so afraid that if I'm not careful, she'll completely take over," or, "Unless I'm really strict, he tries to take over." Now, really. Take over what? The house? The family income? What can a child take over? And why would he want to? I've never met a child in my life who really wanted to reverse roles with his parents and get up every morning and work and pay bills and drive in rush hour traffic and go to dull meetings and have the responsibilities of the adult world.

When questioned about their fear that their child will "take over," most parents admit that what they actually fear is that their child will no longer be obedient. And since they are usually seeking help because the child is in fact already not obedient, they believe their worst fears are being realized and that they are in imminent danger of the child "taking over."

So it is around the issue of obedience that the first problems between parents and children usually arise. The issue of obedience, however, only comes about when parents view their child as a potential enemy from the minute she is born. The battle lines are drawn in many cases in the first few days or weeks of an infant's life, when the parents start defending themselves against what they view as an attempt to "take over" their lives when their infant cries. In homes all across the nation, there are babies lying in cribs screaming in red-faced frustration and misery, while mothers and fathers sit in stoney silence in another room, ignoring their urge to go comfort the baby because they fear "giving in" to the baby's demands. Their need to give comfort, reassurance, love, and nurturance thus becomes twisted into fear of submission and subservience, because parents fear their baby will control them if they give him what he needs and wants when he needs and wants it.

Thus the baby is denied the closeness and warmth of his

parents, and the parents are denied the joy and satisfaction of expressing their love and nurturance toward their baby. They are very often caught up from the beginning in what they view as a continuing struggle for control with a child who is not trying to take control at all, but is trying to find security in a frightening world.

Many pediatricians and child psychologists encourage the battle by describing it as a "power struggle," and parents are often advised to let a baby cry for long periods of time to show him who's boss. Why would a helpless infant who can do nothing but wave his arms and legs about try to gain power over his parents? Isn't that, really, a pretty silly idea? Isn't it far more likely that he simply feels very vulnerable and unsure and uncomfortable and wants some comforting and love?

Imagine that you have had a particularly difficult day at the office. Your supervisor made a veiled threat that your work may not merit a raise when it is due, one of your co-workers was rude to you for no apparent reason, you were totally unable to do your work in an efficient manner, and your morale and feeling of security is at an all-time low. When you come home, you look to your husband for some moral and emotional support, and you tell him about all the trials you have had that day, and you ask him if he would sit with you for a few minutes and hold you.

Imagine how you would feel if he recoiled and said sternly, "You'll just have to suffer alone because if I gave in to your demands, you'd be in control!"

But if the reverse happened, and he lovingly took you in his arms and held you close for a few minutes and reassured you of your worth and value, would you feel that you were in control of him? And is there anybody in the world who would define your request and his refusal as a power struggle? It would more likely be defined as extreme insecurity on his part, with a little paranoia around the edges.

An infant can't verbalize her needs. She can't say, "Listen, you don't know this, but you've put my crib here in this corner and it's gloomy here and a little scarey and I'm bored to death and the detergent you use to launder my clothes causes my skin to sting and I miss the warmth and comfort of the womb where I could always hear your heartbeat and feel close to you, and I just need a little holding and a little loving and in a few weeks, I'll feel safer." All she can do is cry, and if nobody comes she may become frightened and believe that she is totally alone and cry even harder, and turn red in the face from exertion and alarm.

When she's older, around two, she may cry and whine for something to eat before dinner, again because she can't verbalize her feelings adequately. If she could, she would probably say something like, "I *really* am hungry, even though it's not dinner time. My stomach hurts and I don't understand why I have to wait until you're hungry before I can eat, and I believe that if you loved me and cared about me you would feed me now." And it is absolutely meaningless if her mother angrily tells her, "You'll spoil your dinner if you eat anything now, so go watch TV until dinner is ready."

What does "spoil your dinner" mean, anyway? What does that have to do with the fact that she's hungry? If her mother cheerfully feeds her early, before the rest of the family, or if she gives her some bites of cheese or sticks of carrot or celery or a slice of apple to nibble on while she waits to eat with the family, is she controlling her mother? Has she won in some mythical "power struggle," or has her mother simply understood her needs and responded to them in a nonthreatened and rational way?

If you had been adrift on a raft for days and days and had finally been rescued at the point of starvation—which is just about the way a young child feels when he's hungry—and your rescuers were preparing a banquet for you, how would you feel if they refused to give you some small tidbit to eat until the banquet was ready? And if they gave you something beforehand, would you triumphantly feel that you had won in a power struggle, or would you simply be more comfortable and grateful for their understanding?

7

The concept of a "power struggle" between child and parent probably came about because so many adults had parents who believed in it, and the concept is passed down from generation to generation. But can you honestly remember being in a struggle for power with your parents? If you rebelled against them and complained to them and fought them, was it for power over them or was it because you were hurt and angry and confused because they were unwilling to meet your very real needs?

Sometimes a child will be taught by his parents to struggle against them, if the parents always approach the child as if they are afraid he will gain control over them. If a mother abruptly interrupts a child's play to say antagonistically, "Put that away, you have to go to bed now," the child will likely respond with whining or delaying or anger, which will be interpreted as a struggle for control or power, and cause the mother to become angry, with threats, shouting, and punishment.

In most cases, the child is reacting to the mother's tone of voice, which says, "Now get ready for a fight," and to the unfairness of the manner in which the situation was handled. If the mother cheerfully said, "In five minutes, it will be bedtime", the child would be prepared and could start finalizing his play. Or, better yet, if she said, "What story would you like me to read you tonight? I'll help you put your toys away, and then let's go choose a story and I'll read it to you," he would be free of any coercion and could happily and cooperatively get ready for bed and story time. But in neither of those cases would the child be in control of anything, except his own pride. In fact, the mother would be very much more in control than she would be in the first example, when her "control" depended on anger and punishment.

To repeat, your child is not your enemy. She is your friend. She is eager to cooperate with you. She wants to be good, to be cooperative, to be loving and helpful. And if you answer her needs, without some irrational fear that she will "take over" or "control" you, the two of you can have a rich and rewarding relationship in which she will try to be as respectful of your needs as you are of hers.

The child who appears to be in a "power struggle" with his parents is responding to their provocative behavior which invites resistance, and will probably grow up to be just as provocative with his own children, in the belief that they will forever be trying to "take over" if he doesn't firmly deny their needs and punish them severely when they are provoked to rebellion.

You may be thinking that all this is well and good, but what about obedience? Well, what about obedience? What do you mean when you say obedience? Do you want to be able to say "Come!" to your child and have him trot obediently over, wagging his tail? Or do you want to be able to say, "Go to bed!" to your child and have her immediately trot off to bed and curl up and lie down? Do you want to be able to say, "Here, eat this," to your child and have him gobble up every bite and lick the bowl? Remember, we're talking about children, not dogs or cats, and only dogs or cats can be trained to be "obedient" in that manner. Children, being more inquisitive and brighter than animals, are more likely to say "Why?" when given a direct command, and then debate your reason with you.

Just think how terrible it would be if children were as obedient as some parents think they want them to be. They would never learn to think for themselves, they would never learn to make decisions for themselves, they would never progress in their intellectual ability any further than an average housedog or cat, and they could be led and commanded by any dictator or cult leader who came along.

Do you really want a child like that? Or when you say that you want an "obedient" child, do you really mean that you want a child you can lazily care for by remote control? When it's bedtime, a lazy parent can demand "obedience" and order a child to go to bed because it's too much trouble to take her by the hand and lead her to bed and tuck her in and perhaps read her a story or put her favorite record on the record player so that she can listen to music as she drifts off to sleep.

Or a lazy parent can demand "obedience" and order a toddler to put a crystal vase down rather than getting up and gently taking it from him. If the vase is broken, the lazy parent can blame the breakage on the "disobedience" of the child, rather than on her own laziness.

Lazy parents who want remote control of their children are most vocal and evident in department stores, supermarkets, and restaurants. They are the ones who bark commands at their children such as "Put that down!" "Come back here!" "Stop that running!" and "Bring that back to me right this minute!" while they lean on their baskets and visit with friends. After they have barked commands which are ignored, they become infuriated and grab the child and spank him or pinch him or glare at him and tell him through clenched teeth that he will get a whipping later for being "disobedient." The problem is not the child's disobedience, but the parents' laziness.

Little children learn absolutely nothing from being yelled at or ordered about from across the room. They learn by being gently and firmly led or carried. They may not like where they are taken, and they may complain loudly about being taken there, but they will learn that people who are bigger and smarter than they will not allow them to do things that might cause damage to themselves or to property. They can therefore relax and not be afraid that their lack of experience and lack of inner self-control will cause them to be hurt.

Much of the frustration that parents feel when they try to force their children to "obey" is caused by the way they view the problem. If your child is sitting next to you at a table in a restaurant, for example, and is waving his napkin over his head like a flag, you have two or three choices. You can tell him sternly to put his napkin in his lap where it belongs and expect—or hope—that he will "obey." The chances are, of course, that he will simply giggle and continue waving it, in which case you can punish him by slapping his hand or

10

speaking sharply to him, which will probably make him cry and dinner will be ruined for you and everybody else in the restaurant.

Another possible course is to warn him, "If you don't stop waving that napkin, I'm going to spank you," or, "You'll have to go sit in the car," or, "You'll go without dinner." You have thereby given him permission to continue to wave the napkin, and he may do so and take the punishment resentfully, since you allowed him to continue behavior which you disliked and then made him take the responsibility for the behavior.

The easiest and most effective course of action is to stop him from waving the napkin and continue your meal in peace.

The question is, are you more interested in his "obedience," or are you more interested in getting him to quit waving the napkin? If you are more interested in getting him to quit waving the napkin, simply reach out and quietly but firmly take it away from him and place it in his lap. If you do that with a look that says, "I'm not going to discuss this with you, but that napkin stays in your lap," he will probably decide to settle down.

If you are consistent in that type of response, you may not have a totally "obedient" child, but you won't have one who waves his napkin around at the dinner table either. Furthermore, since your child will learn that you simply do not allow some behavior, there will be less temptation for him to attempt it in the future.

Always remember that if you say to a child, "If you do that, I will punish you," you have given him permission to do it. So it is not disobedience if he does whatever you have given him permission to do. You have issued a challenge to him, told him what the consequences will be, and in effect dared him to do it, and he may accept the dare because he will feel humiliated if he doesn't.

Teachers often invite cheating among students by telling them, "If I catch anybody cheating, they will get a zero on their paper." Nobody may have intended to cheat, but when they are challenged to do it without being caught, a lot may try it just to keep from feeling that they have been intimidated.

If you really don't want a thing done, don't allow it to be done. And to prevent any misunderstanding about what you will and will not allow, you can tell your child, "I will not allow you to do that." You don't have to tell her how you intend to stop her, but you have to be absolutely sure in your own mind that you will, even if it means stopping her with a flying tackle in the middle of St. Patrick's Cathedral. If you are really determined to prevent a particular behavior, your child will know it, and will not attempt it since she will know that it's pointless to do so. But if you tell her that you will punish her if she does it, she has a choice.

Look at it this way: If you got a new job and your boss told you that the hours were from nine to five, you would probably accept the hours without question. If, however, the boss said, "If you come to work at noon, we will dock your pay," you might some day choose to sleep late and make less money. It would be bad enough to make less money, but if your boss became angry and accused you of being disobedient, you wouldn't think that was very fair, would you?

When you get right down to it, human beings, including children, only obey those rules or injunctions they want to obey, and they only want to obey those they understand and that seem to have some sound reason behind them. You don't stop at a stop sign simply because the law says you have to, you stop there because you understand the reason behind the law, and you believe that it is essential for safe travel on the streets for everybody to agree to stop at stop signs.

Children, however, have to be at least about ten years old before they can begin to understand the idea of universal agreement which creates a rule or law, and they have to be about four or five before they understand the idea of family unity which causes all the family members to agree on certain types of behavior for the good of the entire family. Until then, they will have to be simply prevented from doing things you don't want them to do, and when they are older they can be told that you expect certain behavior from them and you can expect a reasonable amount of cooperation.

The paradox is that those parents who prevent rather than punish, and who expect cooperation rather than obedience are usually pointed out as models of parents whose children are "obedient." Nobody seems to notice that the good behavior is based on family cooperation rather than on blind animal-like obedience.

I suppose something should be said about spanking, since the relative merits of spanking seem important to so many parents. Spanking gives to some parents the necessary feeling of authority that they otherwise lack, and allows no room for doubt in anybody's mind about who is boss. That's probably the reason that first children are spanked more frequently than subsequent children are. New parents aren't so sure of their own authority, so they rely on spanking to confirm it. As they become more experienced and more confident of their own control of things, they don't need to spank anybody to prove they're in charge.

Children seem to adapt to a parent's need to spank, and they accept spanking as a legitimate form of discipline, so long as the spanking is lightly administered and not too frequent. But while spanking may make parents feel more sure of themselves, and while children may tolerate a reasonable amount of light spankings, their behavior isn't changed by spanking. If the spanking is too hard or too often, in fact, they will actually become more prone to misbehave.

The rationale behind spanking is that if a particular kind of behavior is accompanied by pain it will be less likely to happen again. In some cases, that's true. A child who puts his hand on a hot stove, for example, will be careful in the future to avoid the pain of a burned hand.

The problem of spanking to administer pain during behavior, however, is that the spanking usually comes after the act, and so the child is more likely to associate spanking with the person administering it than he is to associate spanking with the behavior that preceded it. If a toddler goes into the street, he may remember not to go there again if he is spanked immediately while he is still in the street. But if the spanking comes after he's been brought back to the sidewalk, he may associate spankings with sidewalks and not with streets.

It's for that reason that waiting until Daddy gets home or until some private time to administer a spanking may make the parent feel virtuous, but the child will only associate the spanking with the time or place it was administered, and rarely associate his former behavior with it.

If you must spank, be sure that your spankings are very light, with only one or two smart taps on your child's derriere, administered during the behavior you want stopped, and that spankings are very infrequent. When you must resort to spanking a child to punish him for some unwanted behavior, it actually indicates a failure on your part to watch him closely enough and to prevent the behavior rather than allowing it and then punishing him for it.

Most seasoned parents are philosophically opposed to spanking, but remember times when a few well-placed spats cleared the air and allowed tense parents and sulky children to become friends again. Spankings should *never* be administered with belts, straps, whips, or wooden paddles of any sort. A child's body is fragile and can be easily bruised by such treatment. If you find yourself needing to resort to such sadistic beatings, you need professional help at once and should not delay in getting it.

The Swedish government, acting in the belief that all violent abuse against children begins with spanking, recently enacted legislation making it unlawful for Swedish parents to spank their children. A parent who resorts to spanking will be reported to the child welfare authorities, and a counselor will work with the parents to try to change their method of punishment. The Swedes believe that such intervention into families is a part of human rights, and that children, like adults, have the basic human right not to have to live with violence.

14

While it is doubtful that a similar law will ever be passed in this country, it would be very helpful if all parents would re-examine their need to spank, expecially if they find themselves resorting to a light spanking more than once a week.

Your child is not your enemy, and you can trust him and have faith in him and enjoy him without fearing that there are rules of living that you are failing to impart to him. Instead of concentrating on how well he follows commands, look at yourself and see how well you cooperate with other people and how much self-respect you have. Are you always angry, no matter what happens? Do you always have a hopeless, pessimistic attitude, no matter what is going on? Do you feel chronic self-pity because it seems that the rest of the world has been dealt with better than you? Are you always defensive and ready to fight anybody over any little thing?

If any of these things are true, then you will do your child a tremendous favor by getting professional help that concentrates on you and your feelings instead of him and his behavior. If you don't, you're liable to look to your child to make up to you for all you feel you're missing in life, and you'll be disappointed in him when he can't do that. To help your child grow up healthy and whole, you first have to be sure that you're more grown up than he is, and if you're not, do something about it before any more damage is done to either of you. There's nothing to be ashamed of if you have children before you're completely grown up, but there is something to be ashamed of if you stay immature and make no attempt to become an adult before your child does.

There are moments when everything goes well;
don't be frightened, it won't last.
> *-Jules Renard, Journal,*
> 1864–1910

Chapter Two

THEY WON'T STAY MESSY FOREVER
(AND IF THEY DO, IT'S SOMEBODY ELSE'S
PROBLEM)

Having had my standard lecture on the difference between obedience and cooperation, many of you are probably now thinking to yourself, "That's all very well and good, but I have a kid whose room is so sloppy I'm afraid we'll lose him in there someday, his table manners are disgusting and repulsive, he is selfish and inconsiderate, he never returns things he borrows from the rest of the family, his books and clothes and toys are scattered all over the house, he tracks in mud without wiping his shoes, I have caught him in lies, I know he cheats at games, and I don't know where some of the stuff in his room came from, but I'm afraid he stole it. If I don't teach him to obey some rules, he will grow up to be an inconsiderate slob, and he just may be a delinquent."

If you're talking about a fourteen-year-old, you have a serious problem, and your child needs immediate help. If you're talking about a ten-year-old, something is wrong and you're running out of time. But if you're talking about a child between the ages of two and eight, he sounds pretty normal, and there is no need to despair. There is also no need to passively accept your child's undesirable behavior, without laying down some rules which you expect him to follow. In fact, a child who has no rules surrounding him is more apt to feel insecure and inadequate than one who is free to follow his or her own instincts. When a child can relax secure in the knowledge that his parents will decide what is acceptable, and will then provide fair and reasonable boundaries, he can concentrate on the things that are most important to him, like wondering how birds stay on a limb while they sleep, or how pictures fly from a TV studio to a TV set.

So let's take those complaints one at a time, and see why your child–and all children–seem to do the same things to drive parents wild. Messy, cluttered, unsightly–and possibly unsanitary–rooms head the list of every parent's horror stories, but I've yet to meet a child who was uncomfortable in a messy room. A very young child, in fact, is totally unaware of clutter and messiness, and if you scold her for not picking up her toys or for scattering crumbs on her floor, she will become puzzled and hurt because she has no idea what you're talking about. By the time a child is six or seven, he will pick up a few things when told to clean his room, but he will usually forget what he's supposed to be doing, and when he comes across a toy long-buried under debris, he will happily begin to play with it and be hurt and resentful if you suddenly appear in his doorway and yell at him to finish cleaning his room.

By eight or nine, most children will sheepishly admit that their parents are upset because their rooms are messy, but they only make sporadic attempts to rearrange their clutter so that it meets with approval. At this age, it is typical for parents to become wild with frustration when they tell their children to go clean their rooms, only to look in later and see crumpled bits of paper, dirty socks, toys, games, and remnants of unidentifiable food lying on the floor, with a closet full of tangled hangers, rumpled clothes, and a mud castle drying on the floor.

Parents become especially enraged when they angrily confront their child with, "I thought I told you to clean up your room!" and hear an indignant and righteous, "I did!"

To understand the messy-room syndrome, parents have to understand how a child's mind works, and how a child's eyes see. In the first place, there is a direct correlation between a person's size and the amount of space he or she needs around him. Too little space makes a person feel smothered and cramped, but too much space makes a person feel slightly uneasy and vulnerable.

To understand that, imagine how you would feel if you lived in a closet. Unless it was a very large closet, you would quickly become uncomfortable and feel cramped. The larger you are, the larger your closet would have to be in order for you to even tolerate it for a little while. On the other hand, imagine that you lived alone in the middle of a desert. All that space would make you feel terribly insignificant and unimportant. You would probably set to work to drag rocks and prairie dog skeletons around you to make you feel that there was some boundary between you and the vast expanse around you.

When a child is put in a room that is roughly three or four times bigger in all directions than he is tall, his first and natural impulse is to fill as much of that space as he can until he narrows down the void around him to a comfortable boundary. And a child's comfortable boundary depends on his size. Remember that before birth, your child was in very small quarters, snug in the uterus with arms and legs comfortably tucked close to his body. After birth, he felt most comfortable and secure if you wrapped him very snugly in a light blanket, so that he didn't feel that he had been propelled into a tremendous void in which he was totally helpless and vulnerable.

As he grows, he will be able to tolerate a little more space around him. He will enjoy viewing large areas such as the room he's placed in or his yard or the world going by the car windows, but he still feels most secure when he is surrounded by things to put boundaries between himself and the world outside. The stuffed animals and music boxes and mobiles that babies like in their cribs offer not only amusement and stimulation, but also serve to constrict the space around them and make them feel more secure.

By the same token, when your four-year-old piles every toy he owns—even the hard, sharp-pointed ones—into bed with him, he is making himself feel more secure by narrowing down his surrounding space. And when he scatters toys and games and bits of paper on his floor, he's not doing that just to drive you bananas, but to make himself feel more secure and unafraid of the space around him.

With each inch of growth, there is a greater ability to tolerate more space. But even an eight-year-old is a pretty short person, and the amount of space that is comfortable to her will be a fairly small area by adult standards. And even a ten-year-old will feel cozier and safer if there is a lot of furniture, momentoes on the wall, collections on the tabletops, race tracks or doll houses on the floor, and a trail of bits and pieces of trash and treasures decoratively arranged between and upon everything else.

There is usually a period of relative neatness in every child's life that descends around the age of eleven or twelve, when he becomes almost compulsively neat and orderly. He may make his bed with the covers drawn very tightly, and then make a big production of slithering into bed at night and slithering out again in the morning without disturbing the covers. At this stage, he will carefully line up all his pencils, straighten his books on the shelf, tidy his dresser drawers, and generally be a pleasure and delight to his parents. Enjoy that stage when it comes, because it won't last long.

In adolescence, there is a kind of regression, so that an adolescent's need for security may equal that of a four-year-old's, and his room may revert to the messiness and clutter of a four-year-old. Even though he may be growing at an alarming rate, his *psychological* size seems to shrink at this age, and so he responds as if he were very small in physical size. During this stage there are so many other more important matters to contend with that it's usually best to confine your nagging to demands that food and dirty dishes be removed daily from his room in the interest of sanitation, and otherwise leave his room up to him. If you absolutely can't stand the view of a tangled mass of sweaters, books, records, and the other paraphernalia of the young, you are within your rights to insist on a weekly cleaning/organization, but otherwise stay out and don't look.

When adolescents find a romatic interest, their feeling of security usually increases, and their rooms become slightly less sloppy. However, some people remain sloppy and messy, with a need to restrict the space around them, for life. If you've provided a model of orderliness and cleanliness in the rest of your child's home and if you've made reasonable demands for some degree of neatness in his room that is consistent with your child's stage of development, then there's nothing else you can do, and you'll only make yourself and him miserable and frustrated if you let the issue of a clean room become a battleground. If in fact your child does grow up to be one of these people who still have to surround themselves with clutter in order to feel secure, at least you won't have to live with it, and he will be content.

Now, given that you understand why your child is a slob, and given that you don't want to make her feel insecure and anxious by forcing her to live with more empty space than she feels comfortable in, how do you keep her room from becoming a fire or health hazard, and how do you guide her toward the ideal of neatness and cleanliness?

You begin by trying to see her room from her point of view. If she is very small, her bed will seem safer and cozier if it is against a wall than it will in the middle of the room. An alcove with shelves around it on which she can keep her favorite stuffed toys and music boxes will help her to feel safer, too, and if you line her room with low shelves which she can easily see and reach, her world will shrink a little more, and it will be easier to guide her in putting her toys on the shelves.

That arrangement, in fact, will continue to offer security as she grows, and the only alterations that will be necessary will be making everything larger. Most important is that you cheerfully help your child put toys away each day, rather than ordering her to go alone to her room and do it.

If you set the pick-up-toys hour at a time when she is tired and cross, however, and when you are busy and distracted, there is bound to be fireworks and tears and anger. A better time for very small children is sometime in the afternoon when she is happy and rested and when you can help her without hurrying her. This is not a time to put away toys for the day, not to be played with again, but a time to "make your room neat" with the implication that neatness is a positive thing.

Don't be too frustrated if she pulls out every toy again before bedtime. If she does, it probably is because the "neatness" makes her feel uncomfortable and insecure, and not because she wants to see you have a nervous breakdown. Don't scold her, and don't say nasty things like, "Now your room's ugly." That will hurt her feelings, and anyway, beauty is in the eye of the beholder, and in her eyes her room may be much prettier with toys on the floor.

When she is older, you will still have to help her with her room-cleaning. It's unrealistic to expect a child of approximately three feet in height to be able to see all the clutter an adult can see from a higher vantage point. To prove that to yourself, get down on your knees sometime in your child's room, and walk around on your knees and clean and straighten the room until you feel it's in apple-pie order. Now stand up. Unless you've cheated and looked at it first from a standing position and memorized where everything was, you will probably discover something you failed to see while on your knees.

Furthermore, a child's viewpoint is different from an adult's because of the difference in the way children and adults look at things. An adult's eyes scan a room with a sweeping motion, going smoothly from one side of the room to the other, taking in everything that is out of place or incongruous. A child's eyes, on the other hand, look first in one direction and then in another, and take in only those objects which happen to be in his line of vision. Thus, he may see the pile of comic books, and fail to see the orange peels lying a foot away from the books. He may see the empty model-airplane box and fail to see the open tube of glue gently weeping on his dresser top. And he may see all the games and toys on the floor, but fail to take note of the tiny bits of gum wrappers and rubber bands and marbles and tinker toys scattered in the carpet.

Always praise your child when she has made a sincere effort to straighten and clean. Always tell her how well she has done. And always help her a little so it isn't such a disagreeably lonely task. Remember, she's straightening her room to please *you*, not because it bothers *her*. As much as possible, let her do the things she enjoys doing, and help her do the things that are difficult for her. And always, always remember that you are not alone, that your child is normal, and that in millions of homes across America there are children's rooms that are messy and cluttered, and that the child who has a showcase room such as those you see pictured in magazines has a mother or full time maid who does nothing but clean her child's room, and that the child with a spotless room may be less well-adjusted than yours.

Sharing Things You'd Rather Not

While you're helping your child straighten his room, you'll probably come across some things that don't belong there. They may be things that belong to other members of the family, or they may be things that don't belong in your home at all. The matter of children stealing is one that requires a whole chapter by itself, so we'll discuss that later. "Borrowing" things from other members of the family and then not returning them is a different matter.

As a professional trained in child psychology, I can tell you that you can modify your child's behavior so that he will learn to ask for permission before taking things that belong to the rest of the family, and that he can learn to replace borrowed objects in their rightful place. As a mother and grandmother, however, I can tell you that you will never be able to find your scotch tape or your scissors until your youngest child goes off to college. You will save yourself grief and inconvenience if you have a secret hiding place known only to you and God where you keep objects that you absolutely do not want borrowed by anybody anytime.

The concept of ownership, as we will discuss in the later chapter on stealing, is very hazy for children, especially in their very early years. The difference between what is mine and what is thine rarely becomes fixed until a child is about ten years old, and then the distinction between what is a personal possession and what is a possession owned by the entire family usually remains hazy for many years afterward.

Perhaps it should be that way. Perhaps the entire concept of a family is one that should include the idea of possessions belonging in name to one member of a family, but which all other members of the family have some kind of vested right to borrow without formalities. Certainly in every child's mind there are such possessions, and they include such things as scotch tape, scissors, hammers, spoons, string, spools of thread, handkerchiefs, magazines, and umbrellas. To a child, these items are rightfully accessible to every family member, regardless of where they may be kept, and regardless of which family member claims ownership.

Curiously, the same school-aged child who will persistently take spools of thread from her mother's sewing cabinet, in spite of dire threats, punishment, tears, and shouts of outrage from her mother, will not for a moment consider taking a pillow from the living room sofa or a plant from the dining room window. In every child's mind, there are distinctions made between possessions that belong to the house, and are therefore to be left alone, and possessions that belong to another member of the family but are morally okay to use without permission. Unfortunately, most parents don't make the same distinctions, and so the accusations of borrowing things without permission and failing to return them is frequent in most homes.

Almost universally, children continue with a dogged persistence to take "family owned" objects no matter how livid their parents become when they do. They usually look a little nervous and apprehensive when caught and lectured for the three-hundredth time, but it rarely makes them stop. It almost seems that certain parental possessions become symbolical security blankets which a child will continue to use in an almost compulsive manner.

I suppose it is similar to a husband using his wife's hand lotion without permission, or a wife using her husband's binoculars without asking. Intimacy weakens psychological barriers between people and their possessions, and children probably share their parent's possessions because of that same feeling of emotional closeness. Even so, when you're in a hurry to wrap a package, and you have to send out a search party for tape, scissors, paper, and string which have been removed from their proper place, you have to think of some ways to keep your possessions more organized.

Since children own very few things that parents don't use or touch at will, it is very difficult to use the example of, "I don't borrow your things, why do you borrow mine?" You can make that distinction to some extent, however, by buying your child his own roll of tape, his own scissors, some spools of thread, et cetera, and marking them with something like a piece of red tape. Because he will lose his in the clutter of his room, he will still borrow yours unless his are kept neatly with yours.

When you are helping him clean his room, you can direct him to return his scissors, hammer, tape, string, et cetera to the place where these things are kept. When he's older, you and he may discuss where he might keep his own things, but you will have to direct him to replace them while you're helping with the clean up. In time, he will take pride in the fact that he could lay his hand immediately upon his ruler without having to look for it, and that he could immediately find his colored ink pens without an all-day search, but that day won't come until he's almost as tall as you, and you'll make yourself and him miserable and angry if you expect it to come when he's very small.

24

Growing up before your children do

It's Not Poor Memory, It's Selective Memory

Most parents, if asked, would chant in unison, "I don't mind him borrowing things, if he would just remember to put them back where he got them." Remembering to put things away in their proper places, remembering to feed the dog, remembering to empty the wastebaskets, remembering to put the bike in the garage, remembering to turn off the light in the bathroom, remembering to take homework to school, remembering *anything* of importance to parents is another thing that is difficult for the average child.

Ask a child what she had for lunch two hours ago, and her eyes will glaze, her jaw will become slack, and after much effort, she will reply, "I dunno."

Ask her, however, what Mommy said to Daddy last New Year's Eve when Daddy had such a good time at the office party, and she will remember every word. She will remember it so well, in fact, that she may tell it every year at Show and Tell time in school.

And if you are having a casual conversation with a slight acquaintance in the aisle of the supermarket, and you say something like, "We've decided to stay home this year instead of going off on vacation. We have so little time to enjoy just being home, and this year we just decided to relax and read and be quiet instead of rushing around from place to place," trust your child to interrupt with, "That's not why we're staying home, Mommy. Remember, Daddy said we couldn't afford to go anyplace."

Children have remarkable memories for things that you would like them to forget, or at least keep quiet about, and very poor memories for those things that you wish they would remember. A frequent complaint of parents is that no matter how many times they tell a child what his chores are, he will consistently have to be reminded.

Again, to understand and deal with a child's forgetfulness, you have to put yourself in his place. Remember that the world is a remarkable new adventure to him, and that new vistas are opening up to him daily that you have become desensitized to. If a child walks three blocks home from school, for example, his mind is filled with the wonder of the beautiful colors in a puddle of oily water, the thrill of seeing a baby frog so tiny that it fit on his fingernail, the excitement of seeing a police car go by with flashing red lights, the fear of meeting a very large dog that looked mean and angry, the delight of standing transfixed under a shower of falling autumn leaves, and the feeling of importance and pride from having a classmate wave to him with extra friendliness as she turned at her corner to go home. With all that on his mind, how could he be expected to remember something so mundane and dull as wiping his feet, or putting his books in his room, or hanging up his sweater, or any of the other things his parents want him to remember?

When you understand and sympathize with his set of mental priorities, it's easier to help him learn to do the things you want him to do automatically, without having to remember, so that he can continue to think about the things that are really important to him. If you shout at him, "I've told you a million times, dammit, to put your books in your room when you come home!" you won't help him remember to do it, you'll just destroy the happy memories that have been crowding out everything else in his head.

But if you say in a friendly and firm voice, "Hey, let's do that again," and hand him his books, lead him to the door, usher him out and close the door, you will get his attention. He will probably come in grinning, march to his room and put his books away as he's been told a million times to do, and the two of you can then discuss where butterflies go when they die.

Like all effective methods of guiding children along the paths you wish them to take, this method involves some active participation on your part, instead of the lazy way of yelling orders. If you are consistent, patient, friendly and firm, however, the habits you wish to ingrain in him will become second nature, and he will be able to perform routine duties without

26

thinking about them, just as you do.

Repetition, not lecturing, is the key to establishing habits. So if there is anything you wish your child to do habitually, simply guide him repetitiously through the motions until the habit has become ingrained in him. If he always throws his coat on the living room sofa when he comes in the house and you want him to go straight to his closet and hang it up, have him put it back on, go back outside, shut the door, and come in again.

If he always leaves a clutter of paper on the floor when he cuts pictures out of magazines for a homework assignment, and you want him to learn to put the scissors and magazines away and pick up the bits of cut paper, don't yell at him for being inconsiderate and forgetful. Instead, have him go back, sit down, and then get up, throw away the cut bits, neatly replace the magazines, and put the scissors back where they belong. Stay friendly, stay calm, and keep your instructions direct, with no lectures or sermons. If you direct him in the spirit of helping him acquire positive habits, and not in the spirit of humiliating him and punishing him, he will quickly learn the habits you wish him to have, and then both of you can concentrate on things that are more important.

Good Manners Are Caught, Not Taught

The same principle of repetition and respect apply when you are trying to teach your child acceptable social behavior—what we call "good manners." Remember that when you say to a child, "It's not nice to interrupt," she has not the faintest idea what "interrupt" means until she reaches the age of seven or eight. Even then, "interrupt" may mean speaking when another person is talking on the phone, and it may not apply to speaking when two people in the same room are talking. Also, the idea of what is "nice" and what is not nice is hard for a young child to grasp. Ice cream is nice, grandmothers are nice, the next-door dog is nice, but when to talk and when not to talk is a different matter.

It makes more sense to say to a small child, "I cannot listen to you talk until I quit talking." Older children can be told, "This is my time to talk to my friend. I can't talk to my friend and you at the same time." In private, you can discuss talking to different people with your child and tell him that it is called "interrupting" when one person begins to speak while another person is speaking, and that nobody likes to be interrupted.

Help him by praising him when you have had a phone conversation without being interrupted, and when you have had guests without being interrupted. You can say, "Thank you for letting me talk to my friend without interrupting me. I enjoyed my talk, and now I can talk to you."

If you are usually available when your child needs to talk to you and needs your attention, and if you usually put your child's needs ahead of your friend's needs, your child will be more willing to allow you to have uninterrupted time. However, if you escape boredom by incessant chatting on the telephone, your child will feel ignored and abandoned, justifiably so, and will probably interrupt you as much as possible. So before you begin to modify a child's interrupting behavior, be sure that your own behavior is appropriate and not in need of modification.

Most parents, when lecturing their children about good manners, complain about their child's selfishness and lack of consideration for other people. If a child knew the words, he would probably say, "Well, yes, I am selfish, and I am self-centered. That's because I'm a child, and children are egocentric."

We have to always bear in mind that a child's world is extremely small. It begins and ends first in his crib, then in his home, and then in his neighborhood. With no concept of distance or time, whatever happens to a child happens right now, and wherever a child goes is simply where he is.

An infant doesn't imagine where he came from or how long it took to get from one place to another, he simply accepts that there are different people around him and that the surroundings are different. People come and go in his life, and some are more important than others, but he responds to them on the basis of what they do to or for or with him, and he has no thought of doing to or for or with them because of their need or desire.

Gradually, he begins to imitate what other people do, and if his world is filled with friendly, kind people, he will make friendly, kind gestures to others. He will scurry to pick up a dropped object for a grown-up, and proudly hand it to them, beaming when he gets a "Thank you." He will pat his mother's cheek and snuggle up on his father's shoulder, confident that he will be held close and warm. As he grows older, the child whose parents are patient and loving but who firmly guide him where they want him to go will remain affectionate and cooperative, and will try to do things to please his parents. Even then, however, he has to be guided in those acts of generosity or thoughtfulness that we want children to do spontaneously.

It's not fair to expect a child to think of giving gifts or of helping others unless you have given him the idea. A child is simply too egocentric to extend his thoughts to include the idea of another person's pleasure at receiving things from him. You can help your child develop feelings of generosity and thoughtfulness by beginning early in his life to include him in the rituals which you and your family observe, and by encouraging him to personally extend himself.

Don't, for example, buy his grandparents a gift and put his name on it. Instead, encourage him to draw a picture for them, or to paste something together for them. No matter how crudely done his work may be, allow him to present it to them with pride, and he will learn a valuable lesson in giving something of himself to others, as well as experiencing appreciation from others and increasing his sense of personal worth.

When he's older, you will have to prepare him for the fact that holidays or birthdays are coming up, and offer to pay him for extra chores if he wishes to buy something in particular for a friend or loved one. Help him keep his perspective about the purpose of gift-giving by keeping his purchases inexpensive, and encourage him to use his imagination and make things rather than buy things, since his budget is limited. Remember that your child will be as selfish or as considerate as you teach him to be. If he's selfish and inconsiderate, look to your guidance and see how you can better help him learn to think of others.

It's just as important for your child to learn to express appreciation for gifts and favors given to him as it is for him to learn to give of himself to others. But don't be so anxious for him to say the correct "Thank you" that you take away his pleasure and pride in doing so. A child who receives a gift, for example, may smile with pleasure at the giver, only to have his happiness shattered by an impatient tug on his hand from his parent, and a loud "Can't you say 'thank you'?"

He may have been *feeling* "thank you" but not yet have the social confidence to say the words. Or he may have been getting slowly prepared to say the words, and now will feel humiliated and cheated at his parent's coaching. If you want to teach your child the appropriate expressions of appreciation, lean down and unobtrusively whisper them in his ear, so that he won't feel embarrassed by your dictation. If he's too shy to repeat what you tell him, don't make an issue of it. When he's old enough and confident enough, he will remember the correct words and will spontaneously say them.

When he's older, you'll have to remind him to write thank you notes to relatives and friends for gifts, but don't dictate to him what the notes should say, and don't expect him to compose literary masterpieces. The adults who receive the notes will probably cherish them in spite of their deficiencies in legibility and clarity. The important point is for your child to learn to respond with warmth and love to people who care about him enough to remember him with gifts.

Quit Being A Hypocrite About Quitting

Before I conclude this chapter on the criticism that I most frequently hear from parents about their children's behavior, I have to say a word about the complaint that a child is a "quitter." Very frequently I hear a parent say with disappointment and some scorn, "He never finishes what he starts," or "She's like my sister—a quitter."

If a child joins a softball league, for example, and then halfway through the season wants to quit, the parents usually begin to lecture her about the virtues of finishing what she starts. The fact is that nobody knows beforehand whether or not they will like anything, and many of us have found ourselves in a class or a club or a social situation that we expected to enjoy and found that we intensely disliked. Children have even less experience than we have in judging what they will and will not like. It's to be expected that they may rather frequently experiment with new things and then find that the new hobby or sport fails to hold their interest, or that they are inept at whatever they're trying to do and would prefer doing something for which they have a natural aptitude. They may stop doing the thing they don't like and do something else. When adults do that, they call it "eliminating stress," but when children do the same thing, we call it being a "quitter."

To be sure, there are situations in which we must finish what we start, no matter how much we may dislike it. If the rest of the team would be at a disadvantage to lose a member, then the season has to be played out, and played to the best of one's ability and with good grace, simply because it would be unfair to the other members of the team to quit.

Hobbies are a different matter. A child may start a hobby for a lot of different reasons, just as adults do. He may have a friend who enjoys the hobby and he thinks he would too. He may view the hobby as a symbol of prestige in his peer group. He may simply be bored and want something new in his life. Or somebody may give him a gift that starts him on a hobby which he never thought of before.

The difference in the hobbies that children have and the hobbies that adults have is that nobody nags adults to continue theirs, and nobody views it as a character defect if they lose interest in a hobby they once found fascinating.

Remember those demitasse cups you started collecting when you were a teenager? Remember how you wanted to collect them because your best friend had about fifty of them, and they looked so nifty and sophisticated in that special display case in her room? Where are the two or three now that you collected? When did you lose interest? Was it when you started going steady with what's-his-name, or was it when you realized that you really didn't get excited when you opened a birthday gift and found it was a little dinky cup and saucer?

Or, where is the darkroom equipment of yesteryear? Is it still moldering on the garage shelf, or did you secretly slide it into the trash the last time you moved, with a painful memory of the amount of money you spent on it in that flush of enthusiasm when you decided to become another Ansel Adams? Are you guilty of a weak character or of a bad decision? For that matter, where are all those cameras with all the expensive gizmos that you bought at the same time you bought the darkroom equipment? Is it your child whom you fear is an elementary school *dilettante*, or is it yourself you're kicking when you lecture him about finishing what he begins?

A small child may very appropriately flit from one activity to another. She may play awhile with clay, then paint awhile, then build with blocks for awhile. When she's ready to go outside and play with friends, she may leave behind her an unfinished clay model, an unfinished picture, and an unfinished block construction. That's why it's called *play*. She's not a professional sculptor or artist or construction engineer. She's been *playing* at being those things, and there's no moral obligation to finish things that are only play. If there were, it wouldn't be play, but work.

Both play and hobbies are media for self-expression for

children, not tests of endurance and persistence. If you lecture your child and moralize about the importance of finishing everything he begins, you will not only take all the fun out of play, but you will deny him a valuable avenue of self-expression. An older child who has become involved in a short-term group project can be helped to see it through if you are sympathetic to his discomfort in it, but mindful of his obligation to the group. As soon as a particular group project is completed, however, he should be allowed to terminate his association with the group with no hard feelings from his parents or from the group.

If you continue throughout your child's life to teach him cooperation by being cooperative, to teach him consideration by being considerate, and to teach him self-control by providing fair and consistent parental control, you will probably come out on the other side of his childhood and look around with relief and pride, and say to him, "You know, I'm very lucky to have a kid like you!" And you'll be right.

All happiness depends on a
leisurely breakfast
                    -John Gunther

Chapter Three

SOMEONE HAS TO PLAN THE MEALS,
AND YOU'RE THE ONE

I'm now going to do what a neighbor of mine calls "going from preachin' to meddlin'" about children whose minds and spirits and bodies are being harmed by the attitude our society has toward food.

Today's child is being robbed of good nutrition by greedy food manufacturers who have stripped wholesome food of its perishable nutritive value and then processed it with harmful chemicals and dyes in order to extend its shelf life and to make it easier and cheaper to store for long periods of time. As if that weren't bad enough, we also have school districts which allow nonnutritive junk food to be served in school cafeterias or sold in school-owned vending machines. All too often, furthermore, children have parents who are not aware of the nutritional needs of a developing mind and body and who have never read a book or attended a class on nutrition.

All of these distressing situations contribute to the fact that we have a generation of children who are alarmingly prone to hyperactivity, learning disabilities, difficulties in concentration, and to emotional distress such as irritability, fatigue, and over-aggressiveness. I do not for one minute believe that *every* hyperactive child, *every* learning disabled child, or *every* emotionally distressed child is suffering from an improper diet, but many such children are, and in many children the relationship is a causal one.

The most dramatic demonstration I've seen of the effect of food on behavior was the case of Jason, a seven-year-old whose parents and teachers had abandoned hope that he would ever behave or learn normally. The first time I saw Jason was memorable. When I opened the door to the waiting room, it looked as if a tornado had recently passed through. Lampshades were tipsily leaning, magazines were torn and strewn over furniture and floor, and sofa and chair cushions were loose and askew. The pictures on the walls were tilted, and Jason was perched like a restless bird on the back of a sofa making shrill crowing noises.

During a hectic testing session, Jason sailed test material over my head, ran around the room, walked on the furniture while singing that he could fly, and was so distracted by every item in the office that he barely attended to the test. The results were inconclusive, of course, and the only definite statement that could be made was that he was extremely hyperactive and unable to control his own behavior.

Jason was placed on an elimination diet and his tired and hopeless parents were told to bring him back in two weeks. The change in him two weeks later seemed nothing short of miraculous. Jason sat calmly and quietly in the waiting room and then talked rationally and appropriately when he came into my office. He spoke with sadness about his lack of friends and about his recent expulsion from the first grade because of his disruptive behavior.

His parents were ecstatic over the change in Jason, and reluctant to add foods back to his diet. Grimly aware that his former behavior would return, they steeled themselves and started the process of adding back one food at a time to his diet. His mother telephoned after orange juice was returned to his daily food intake, and the background whoops and crashes were enough to let me know that she had identified at least one food that Jason was allergic to. Luckily, orange juice was the only offender, and so long as Jason avoided it he remained calm. If he drank so much as a small glass, however, he turned into a small terror.

Although Jason needed psychotherapy for a while to help heal the emotional scars he had acquired as a result of being rejected by classmates, he gained appropriate social and academic skills in time, and continued to learn and develop in a normal manner. If Jason had been seen ten years sooner, prior to the time food allergies and their effect on behavior were recognized, he might very well have been placed in a psychiatric hospital because of his bizarre behavior.

There are many parents who have drastically changed their children's diets and thereby drastically changed their behavior, but far too many children continue to consume a diet which not only does very little to encourage good mental and physical development, but in some cases is actually detrimental to their health.

Consider, for example, the typical daily diet of many children in America. For breakfast, they may grab a slice of bread or eat a bowl of colored, presweetened cereal and drink a coke while their parents sleep or blow-dry their hair. If they eat lunch in the school cafeteria, they will get a fairly well-balanced meal, but the chances are that it will contain a large amount of refined sugar and white flour. Their after school snack is likely potato chips or cookies, ice cream or coke, and dinner may consist of a macaroni casserole prepared from a packaged mix containing a tongue-twisting mixture of chemicals and dyes.

How did we get into this fix, anyway? How did we become a nation hooked on rancid potato chips and cola drinks? Whatever happened to good food? Whatever happened to an awareness of what good food was?

The answer, of course, is urbanization and "progress." When people moved to the cities from the farms, they could no longer gather fresh eggs for breakfast, or carve a slice of farm-cured ham to go with them, or slice a piece of whole-grain bread to top with a pat of home-churned butter. Instead, at the market they bought infertile eggs that were pale, tasteless, and of suspicious age, and tried to enjoy them along with a slice of commercially cured ham or bacon whose flavor was subtly but definitely altered by the addition of nitrites and nitrates for shelf life. To this disappointing breakfast they added a slice of commercial white bread that had all the flavor, texture, and nutritive value of a handful of blanket fuzz.

The bologna sandwiches they took to work in their lunch boxes were soggy and unsatisfying, and they were too hungry at dinnertime to be appeased with a bowl of oatmeal and some stewed fruit, as they might have eaten back on the farm. Instead, they took to eating large meals at night of heavy pastas and dried beans or peas which were filling and helped stop the grumbling of stomachs accustomed to a large midday meal of fresh fried chicken, fresh vegetables, and just-given milk.

After a while, appetites that had looked forward to real food became jaded, and people who had formerly enjoyed food lost interest and began to eat whatever was handy, and to seek out packaged foods which provided texture or spice or color to distract from the lack of natural flavor. Crunchy potato and corn chips, heavily sweetened and sticky candy bars, packaged desserts, breakfast cereal that snapped, crackled, and popped, caffeine-containing soft drinks, glazed doughnuts, and canned soups and stews began to replace fresh food. The flat, empty taste of prepared foods was disguised by the addition of sugar and more sugar, and the inane white bread was made more palatable by smearing it with commercial jellies and jams.

When somebody occasionally tried to recapture the old pleasures of eating fresh vegetables or fruits, they all too often bit into something such as a tomato picked green and reddened by being exposed to gases, creating a mushy, tasteless vegetable. Apples, cucumbers, pears, and other fruits and vegetables were waxed to give them a shine, and the hungry person who remembered how food used to taste on the farm quite likely drowned his memory by eating a banana split in which the only natural ingredient was the banana.

Many of our children, the grandchildren or great-grandchildren of a rural-turned-urban generation, have never experienced the taste of real food, and neither have many of their parents. The surprise a child or adult feels when first tasting a home-grown tomato or eating a slice of freshly baked whole grain bread is almost pathetic in a nation that so proudly proclaims its superiority in well-stocked supermarkets and in rapid food distribution.

We have become so totally dependent on commercial food processors that it is virtually impossible now to find any food that has escaped the influence of artifical chemicals. At the supermarket, we run the risk of purchasing meat that contains antibiotics or growth-inducing hormones, and it's almost certain the vegetables and fruits we purchase have been subjected to toxic insecticides. Because whole grains turn rancid after a time and cost more to store, the nutritive core is removed during processing, leaving only the hulls, so the cereals, breads, and pastas we purchase have usually been stripped of all nutritive value in the milling or processing. The fact that these processed grains are "enriched" by the addition of artificial vitamins does not give them the same nutritive value whole grains have with their natural vitamins and accompanying trace minerals.

While we all may deplore the present situation, few of us have the temperament, talent, or wherewithal to live on a farm and produce our own food. Our only hope is that consumer demands will cause food manufacturers to create more nutritious food to be sold in supermarkets, and that growers will develop methods of harvesting produce when it is flavorful and still manage to get it to the customer before it spoils. In the meantime, we will probably have to resort to baking our own bread and planting tomatoes among the zinnias if we are to experience truly flavorful food.

The fact that it is impossible for most of us to grow our own food does not get parents off the hook as those responsible for their children's nutrition, however, and I want you to listen closely because this is terribly important:

It is your responsibility to see that your children have nutritious, wholesome, appetizing food every day, three hundred and sixty-five days a year. It is also your responsibility to learn as much as possible about nutrition and about vitamins and minerals and calories and carbohydrates so that you can help your children grow physically and mentally. A malnourished child cannot learn well, she cannot concentrate well, nor can she relate to other people well. And malnourished doesn't mean skinny. A child may be plump and soft and still be suffering from malnutrition. In fact, a child whose diet is heavily loaded with sweets and carbonated drinks is very likely to be both undernourished and overweight. The empty calories of sugar, candy, cakes, soft drinks, fruit-flavored drinks, jellies, jams, potato chips, corn chips, and the like will create a chubbiness which may look healthy, but without adequate protein and other nutrients there will not be proper brain or central nervous system development.

Somehow the word "nutrition" has taken on a negative connotation. Otherwise intelligent, sensible people have a hazy understanding of what "nutrition" is and are slightly hostile to the word. Telling a parent that she needs to pay more attention to her child's nutrition is likely to get a response such as, "He drinks lots of milk, and that's good for him." Or, "I try to get him to eat more, but he won't."

"Nutrition" refers to the process by which a living organism—such as your child—assimilates food and uses it for growth and for replacement of tissues. Nutritious foods such as meats, vegetables, fruits, cereal grains, and dairy products aid growth and development, while the foods that don't contain nutrients simply take up space in the stomach, kill the appetite for nutritious food, and cause excess weight gain from the calories they contain.

Almost every person who has attended elementary school in the United States has been in contact with a nutrition chart showing all the various whole food groups from which a person's diet should be chosen. It's probably not so important to remember those food groups as it is to remember that popsicles are not included in any of them. Nor is Kool-aid or any other colored or sweetened beverage or dessert. And the "cereal" group doesn't refer to the presweetened and colored breakfast cereals which are touted during the Saturday morning cartoon shows. Instead it means whole grain cereals such as rice, oats, wheat, or whole grain breads.

The point is that the foods your child eats can either provide a lot of calories and very little else, or they can provide calories plus many vitamins and minerals. If you purchase a book or two on nutrition, you can become an expert at providing your child with the best possible diet.

Knowing about nutrition and doing something about it, of course, are two different things, which brings me to another favorite preachment: *It is your responsibility to get up in the morning and prepare breakfast for your child.* It is your responsibility for the same reason that it is your responsibility to wash behind your own ears—because you're the adult.

When your children are grown up and getting up with *their* children, you can try to arrange it so that you can be lazy and self-indulgent, but until that time, their nutrition and enjoyment of food is your responsibility, and how well and how cheerfully you carry out that responsibility will have a great deal to do with your child's total development.

Getting up and preparing breakfast and seeing your child off to school is not only important in terms of his nutritional needs, but also because of his emotional needs. Knowing that you care enough about him to prepare a delicious meal in the morning, sit with him and chat about the coming day before he leaves in the morning, and send him off with a cheerful face and a hug will give him a warm glow that will go with him throughout the day. He will be more attentive in class, he will be more cooperative and helpful, and he will be less likely to have constricting feelings of anxiety or abandonment that could interfere with his learning.

In study after study, it has been clearly demonstrated that children who eat wholesome, nutritious breakfasts perform much more efficiently at school, make better grades, have better conduct, have fewer absences from school, get along better with their peers, and are generally happier with themselves than are children who skip breakfast or who have a doughnut and a glass of chocolate milk for breakfast. Short of illness or incapacitation, there is no excuse to fail to give your child that good start every day. If you have to get yourself off to work and your hair has to be shampooed and dried while your child is getting ready for school, get up thirty minutes early and do your hair before you get breakfast for him. If you're always running around hunting your shoes or your purse or your car keys in the morning and leave as your child does, get all those things together the night before, have a leisurely morning with your child, and you will both benefit throughout the day.

If you wake up some morning with fever, sore throat, and a terrible headache, of course, don't drag your sick body into the kitchen in the martyred belief that you have to prepare breakfast for your child at all costs. He won't die if one morning he has to pour himself some juice, toast a slice of bread, and spread some peanut butter on it, and there's no need to lie in bed feeling guilty and worried. It's only when you lie in bed every day because you're too lazy or too tired or too sleepy to get up while your child prepares a makeshift breakfast that you need to examine which of you is the adult and which is the child.

It isn't necessary to become a fanatic or a bore about good nutrition, but it is important for you to have a clear understanding of the difference between whole foods and processed foods, and between natural foods and foods with additives. Don't rely on television commercials to teach you how best to give your child nutritious food. Remember that the "mother" on the TV commercial who gushes about how wholesome Twinkies are is selling something. Did you ever see a commercial for an apple? Probably not often, but there are lots of commercials for apple-filled tarts and the like. You may add to a company's revenue if you buy the prepared apple-flavored sweet snack, but if you're interested in your child's health, buy the apple instead.

I don't intend to go into the subject of vitamin supplements in this book, except to say that it's a good idea to read the minimum daily requirements for all necessary vitamins and minerals and then compare them to the actual vitamin and mineral content of your typical diet. If you conclude that you would have to eat far more food than you do, with far more variety, in order to obtain even the *minimum* necessary nutrients from your diet alone, then vitamin supplements are valuable. Since there are individual differences in the minimum daily requirements of vitamins and minerals, with most people probably requiring more or less than the average, I strongly suggest that you as a parent become thoroughly acquainted with all the pro and con arguments regarding vitamin supplements and then make up your own mind.

And I won't even try to entice you to try baking bread, although if you tried a very simple recipe for whole grain bread, baked with honey, vegetable salt, and vegetable oil, and liberally slathered while it's hot with sweet butter or vegetable margarine, I think you'd be hooked and not mind the half hour a week it takes to mix and knead a couple of loaves of bread. If you haven't the time or desire to bake your own, look for some specialty bakeries or natural food restaurants which sell bread baked with whole ingredients and introduce your children to real bread.

The important point is that parents have the responsibility of getting up in the morning and preparing breakfast for their children with a smile, and either preparing their school lunch or knowing what kind of lunch they eat at the school cafeteria, and preparing a nutritious, tasty dinner in the evening, served with no hassles, no arguments, and no punishment.

If you don't assume that responsibility, then you have to assume the responsibility for children who may have difficulty learning, whose physical growth may be slow, with flabby muscle tone and marginal emotional control, and who may very well suffer from various behavioral problems due to malnutrition or food allergies.

In this particular area, there's not enough time for your children to wait for you to grow up. It's now or never for their nutritional needs, and if you're not quite grown up yet, find some other area to be immature in, but be grown up about their nutrition.

The Food They Like Best May Not Like Them

Good nutrition is especially important for children with learning disabilities or behavior problems. There is overwhelming evidence that many learning and behavior problems are directly related to a cerebral food allergy, or to an allergy to one of the chemicals used in processing modern foods. (A "cerebral" food allergy is one which may not cause any skin rash or other visible signs, but may cause swelling of cerebral blood vessels or other cerebral changes which affect the way the brain or nervous system functions.)

In my own practice, there have been dramatic changes in the hyperactive behavior of some youngsters when sugar was completely removed from their diets. Children who were formerly so jittery and disorganized that they were unable to listen, remember, concentrate, and learn have changed into calm, rational, cooperative youngsters who themselves report feeling much "nicer" and who are in control of themselves as they have not been before.

There have been so many studies demonstrating the effects of sugar on the behavior of some children that there are few doubts that sugar causes a chemical reaction in some children which interferes with smooth neurological functioning. To be sure, there are children who can eat sugar with no apparent ill effects, and some hyperactive children are not changed when sugar is removed from their diet, so the relationship between sugar and hyperactivity or learning disabilities is not clear. It's also not clear why some youngsters react violently to sugar or dextrose and not to honey or fructose. Since hydropetrocarbons are used in the refining process of sugar, it is possible that traces of the chemical remain in refined sugar and that some children are more sensitive to it than others.

Parents frequently remember that when they were children, they ate ice cream and cookies and pies and jellies, and had no learning problems or hyperactivity. More than likely today's children would be able to tolerate the same amount of sugar their parents ate with no ill effects. The problem is that today's processed foods are saturated with refined sugar, and by the time a child is six or seven years old, he has probably consumed twice the amount of sugar his parents had consumed by the time they married.

Sugar until recently has been added to most canned baby food, and it is present in one form or another in bacon, ham, luncheon meats, bread, sandwich spreads, canned soup, many canned vegetables and fruits, fruit juices, carbonated drinks, crackers, frankfurters, and sausage, as well as in the frankly sweet products such as cookies and ice cream. You can spot the parents who have put their children on a sugar-free diet, in fact, by the way they read each label in the supermarket as they move down the aisles, desperately searching for products without dextrose or sucrose or sugar listed on their labels.

Sugar is not the only culprit in the kitchen. Citrus fruits, dried beans and peas, wheat, corn, milk, chocolate, and artificial colors and flavorings have been often implicated in a child's learning or behavior problems. Almost any food, in fact, can cause an allergic reaction in a given child, and the only way to determine if a child has a cerebral allergy to a given food is to remove the food and observe the child's behavior.

Dr. William Crook, a nationally recognized pediatrician and allergist, has done extensive research in the "hidden" cerebral allergies which plague many children and may cause fatigue, irritability, stuffy nose, headache, stomachache, leg ache, pallor, circles under the eyes, bed-wetting, bowel disorders, and behavior and learning problems. Dr. Crook has demonstrated that food allergy tests do not always indicate the presence of a food allergy, and that an elimination diet is the only way to conclusively discover the presence of hidden food allergies.

Dr. Crook recommends a starting elimination diet which avoids milk, chocolate, and cola drinks. If there is no improvement on that diet, he then recommends eliminating for one week any food eaten more than one or two times a week, along with sugar, milk, eggs, wheat, corn, chocolate, citrus fruit, and all food colors and dyes.

Sometimes a child will display "withdrawal" symptoms and feel cranky, tired, and irritable for the first two or three days, but by the fifth, sixth, or seventh day there should be some evidence of improvement. Some children, however, show no significant improvement until the offending food has been eliminated from their diet for as long as two or three weeks.

Another pediatrician and allergist, Dr. Ben Feingold, has achieved similar results by eliminating all synthetic food colorings and flavorings—along with fruits and vegetables containing natural salicylates—from the diets of hyperactive, learning disabled children. There are offices in many cities which provide parents with copies of the Feingold diet, as well as listed sources for markets selling natural foods.

From studying the work of both these physicians, the conclusion seems that some children react to synthetic food additives, while others react to the food itself, and some react to both or neither. Since allergies are such elusive and complicated phenomena, it is not surprising that different individuals have different responses to given factors. A child's heredity, his general health, his emotional equilibrium, his age, the presence or absence of pollens, house dust, pollutants, animal danders, irritants which come into contact with his body, the atmospheric pressure in which he lives, as well as the temperature of his particular geographic location, all contribute to whether or not he will develop allergies.

Putting a child on a diet to determine which, if any, foods might be causing hyperactivity, emotional problems, or some other behavorial symptom such as bed-wetting or stomach cramps is a tricky task. First, you have to get yourself mentally set, and that may take a week or more just thinking about it and planning all the alternative foods that your child might eat while on an elimination diet. Since children usually crave the very foods that cause them problems, they will often be touchy and disagreeable for the first few days of an elimination diet, and they will sneak forbidden foods if they are available. It's best, therefore, to time the diet to coincide with a time when you or another adult can carefully monitor the diet, and when nothing of particular importance is going on in your child's world.

It's also important for the rest of the family to go on the same diet with the child so there is no temptation for the child to eat forbidden food. The child should feel that the diet is a family affair, and not something intended to punish him.

You must have a very clear understanding of exactly which foods you plan to eliminate, and why, and you must be absolutely certain that there are no lapses. Don't try to switch back and forth between various elimination diets, but choose one and stick to it until you see a change in your child's behavior, which usually occurs in one to three weeks.

After the seven to twenty-one-day trial and an improvement in the child's behavior, one food at a time can be added back, allowing a day or two between each new addition. If the child's behavior improves after the first seven days, and then drastically deteriorates after a particular food has been reintroduced, that food is at least one of the foods he should not eat, and it should be withdrawn again and other foods returned one at a time, with each food that causes a reaction withdrawn again. It takes approximately three days for a food's traces to be completely eliminated from the body, so wait about three days after a reaction before adding back another food.

The problem with this method of eliminating possible allergens from the diet is that it causes shock to most families, with resulting irritability and hollow eyed looks of deprivation. I have found that it sometimes works as well, although it takes a much longer time, to string out the process of elimination and to only eliminate one or two foods at a time. Sugar or milk, for example, can be eliminated for a period of one to three weeks without creating a drastic change in a family's eating habits. Eliminating either of these two foods will require intense watchfulness and care when purchasing any canned, packaged, or frozen foods. Dried milk solids are added to breads, soups, meats, and other foods with almost the same frequency as sugar, so one must read labels religiously to avoid inadvertently eating something that contains sugar or milk. If you eliminate milk, you'll also, of course, have to omit cheese and cheese foods, along with butter, sour cream, whipped cream, ice cream, sherbet, cream gravy, and a lot of other dairy foods that you may habitually eat. Caseinate containing "non-dairy" cream substitutes and whipped toppings must also be eliminated, since Caseinate is a milk protein.

If you eliminate eggs, remember that macaroni, noodles, many sauces, marshmallows, meat loafs, croquettes, custards, hamburger mixes, ice creams and icings, and many other mixed foods contain eggs.

Similarly, if you are eliminating corn, avoid corn syrup, corn sugar, corn oil, corn starch, and corn oil margarine. Corn is also apt to be in candies, cereals, carbonated drinks, chewing gum, peanut butter, pastries, pork and beans, puddings and sherbets, and many other mixed foods.

Since cola drinks are made from cola nuts, a relative of the cocoa bean, all cola drinks should be avoided when eliminating chocolate, but other carbonated drinks can be drunk. Children can remember that the "white" carbonated drinks are permitted.

Sometimes children are allergic to legumes, which include peas, beans, peanuts, and soybeans. If you are eliminating legumes, avoid soybean oil margarine, soy sauce, peanut butter, and any breads, baked goods, cookies, sauces, and candies that contain legume products.

Unsuspected food allergies are usually discovered by other family members when the entire family joins a child in eliminating one or two foods at a time for one to three weeks. Many parents who have chronic nasal congestion, headaches, stomachaches, or insomnia discover they feel much better when they leave off sugar or milk or one of the other frequent offenders.

If there is no change in a child's behavior after one to three weeks of eliminating one or two foods from his diet, and if you are absolutely sure that you have carefully read every label of every processed food he has eaten and that he has not cheated when he was out of your sight, add them back to his diet and go on to another pair of foods.

After eliminating every possible food that might be causing an allergy, along with all artificial colors and flavors, if there is still no change in your child's behavior, you'll have to try the diet which eliminates all the possible offenders at the same time, rather than stringing it out one food at a time. The problem may be that the child is allergic to several foods and that his behavior does not improve when one of them is removed because others are still present. It's usually easier for the family to tolerate the complete elimination diet after experiencing eliminating one food at a time. They'll be accustomed to diet changes and will usually not feel so deprived as they do when the change is sudden and drastic.

These elimination diets, of course, should be considered only if your child has any symptoms of a food allergy. Remember that food allergies are not only manifested in rashes or hives, but also in fatigue, irritability, learning difficulties, hyperactivity, stomachaches, headaches, leg aches, urinary or bowel disturbances, circles under the eyes, pallor, runny or stuffy nose, frequent ear infections, excessive sweating, drowsiness, nervousness, and a host of other symptoms.

If your child has none of these symptoms, there's no need to start eliminating food from his diet simply because some other children have food allergies. However, you can help prevent the occurrence of food allergies by serving a wide variety of whole foods, especially vegetables, fruits, whole grain cereals, lean meat, eggs, nuts and seeds, and a moderate amount of dairy products. Avoid all prepared and artificially flavored and colored foods, and strictly limit the amount of sugar, cola drinks, white flour and fat your child consumes. If he is generally healthy, learns well and has no signs of emotional distress, an *occasional* cola drink or a snowcone dyed red and flavored with cane syrup probably will cause no harm other than a higher incidence of tooth decay. A steady diet of such foolishness, however, is harmful.

To learn more about allergies and their effect on children, read Dr. Crook's books, *Can Your Child Read? Is He Hyperactive?* and *Your Child And Allergy*, available from Professional Books, P. O. Box 3494, Jackson, Tennessee 38301; and Dr. Feingold's book, *Why Your Child is Hyperactive*, published by Random House.

Food Goes With Smiles, Not Frowns And Fights

How *much* a child eats is far too often a source of conflict between child and parent, and the conflict frequently follows a child throughout her life, creating weight problems or an inability to enjoy food. The obsession with how much a child ate was never much of a problem in the days when a child nursed at the breast until the next baby came along, and then ate from the table as little or as much as he wanted. Between-meal snacks were less likely to be an appetite-depressing sweet, and children were assumed to be able to judge for themselves how much and what they should eat.

With the popularity of bottle-feeding came an awareness on the part of the mother of the number of ounces of milk that a baby had consumed, and mothers began to compete with one another.

A baby who nurses at his mother's breast, of course, may spend five minutes swallowing milk, consuming approximately six ounces, and another ten minutes suckling for the fun of it, without the mother's awareness of when the milk supply dwindled. But if a mother fills a baby bottle with eight ounces and the baby only takes six, the instinctive reaction on the part of many mothers is to try to encourage the baby to drink the remaining two ounces, on the theory that more is better.

Thus the stage can be set for future struggles as the mother tries to dictate to the child how large his stomach is and what amount of food is satisfying to him. Children with such mothers usually rebel and develop bizarre food preferences, or throw up when urged to eat a new food, or make mealtime so unpleasant for the entire family with their whining that everyone wishes they would just shut up and not eat at all.

I remember one four-year-old child who would eat fried chicken legs and fried potatoes and sliced white bread, period. He would not eat fried chicken breasts or wings or thighs or any other part of the chicken. He would not eat mashed potatoes or boiled potatoes or baked potatoes, and he would not eat bread if it was toasted. He screamed in rage and frustration if he did not have those three foods at every meal, and he would not eat any other food in spite of pleas and threats and bribes and punishment from his harried and angry mother.

Every meal was filled with fights and shouts and tears, and the child sometimes went to bed hungry because his mother refused to prepare his favorite food, and he refused to eat any other. Their struggle over the food he ate was exhausting to both, and it permeated their entire relationship. They glared at each other between meals, and they were tense and apprehensive at all times, anticipating the next mealtime struggle.

At my suggestion, the mother fried a large number of chicken legs and froze them. She also fried some potatoes and made a quantity of individual frozen servings. And at every meal she heated a frozen fried chicken leg and a portion of fried potatoes and served them to him with a slice of untoasted white bread. She made no comment, and she prepared other food for herself, and sat down with him and calmly ate it. Before dinner, they chose a record to listen to while they ate, and the child helped in the selection. They ate together, listening to the music, and there was no more conflict over the child's menu.

After a week or so, he asked her one evening if he could have a bite of her macaroni and cheese. She gave him a very small portion without comment, and he ate it greedily. (He was probably so tired of fried potatoes and fried chicken legs by this time that he would have enjoyed baked cardboard.) At the next meal, he asked for a bite of canned fruit from her plate, and she again shared it with him without making any suggestions or comments, and without urging him to eat more.

At each meal thereafter, he continued to ask for food from her plate, and she finally said, "I'll give you some of your own." She gave him a very *small* portion on his plate, and he ate it happily, and ignored his fried chicken leg and fried potatoes entirely.

At the next meal, she prepared two plates of food for him, one with the fried chicken leg and fried potatoes, and another with the same food she was eating, but in much smaller portions. She showed him both plates and asked, "Which dinner would you prefer?" Probably relieved to change his diet, he asked for the new food, and their former conflict over food never came up again.

While this was an extreme case, the point is that food is eaten for nutrition and enjoyment, and not to please somebody else. If your child howls every day for a food that is nutritionally sound, and which can be prepared in quantity and served in individual portions, let him have it. So long as his overall nutritional needs are met, don't be alarmed by a fanatic demand for some favorite. Even if his diet is not balanced daily, he will probably get a good balance over a period of several days if his only choices are meats, eggs, vegetables, fruits, cereals and dairy products, with no junk food included.

Also, don't get so hung up on one food that is a favorite of yours that you make your children miserable with your demands that they eat it. It may be the most nutritious food in the world, but if your children hate it, another food they like would be a far better choice.

51

Growing up before your children do

I once knew a woman who regularly whipped her children with a belt because they refused to eat oatmeal for breakfast. They loved cream of wheat and would have happily eaten it, but she believed they should eat what she cooked, whether or not they liked it. So every morning she cooked oatmeal, they refused it, and she lined them up with their pants down and made them hold their ankles while she self-righteously whipped them with a broad leather belt. It seems unbelievable that such sick and immature behavior could happen in even one home, but the fact is that there are many homes in which food becomes such a point of contention that permanent damage is done to the children. Always, the parents who are abusing their children over food do so in the proclaimed belief that they are being "good parents," and that their only interest is in "good nutrition."

Some children are forced to sit at the table until they consume every bite of their food, even if they must sit for hours, and even if they finally throw up the food once they have swallowed it. Other children are not forced to remain at the table with uneaten food, but are served the uneaten food at the next meal and the next, until it is finally eaten.

I know one child who was served the same cold, dismal liver for several meals until she finally gulped it down with shuddering sobs, threw it up, and was then allowed to eat food that she liked. She knew, however, that liver would be served at least once a week in her home, and that she would eat it at the meal when it was served or have it presented to her at every following meal until she ate it. Her mother believed she was practicing "good nutrition" by forcing her daugher to eat hated liver because she knew liver was rich in iron and Vitamin B. She defeated her own purpose, however, by force-feeding her child, and it was not surprising that her daughter developed numerous food phobias and was dangerously underweight.

Many parents use the strategy of "you have to eat everything you put on your plate" in the foggy notion that they are somehow teaching their children a lesson in etiquette or thrift or advance planning. These are the same parents who tell their children about the starving people in India or Bangladesh, and try to induce guilt feelings in their children if they fail to eat everything on their plates. In actual fact, of course, what they are doing is punishing their children for being inconsiderate of others and taking more food than they actually need, thus depriving someone else of it. A better manner of teaching the same lesson is simply to stop a child from taking more than a modest amount of food, with the promise of seconds if he or she wants more.

Some insecure parents are identified with the food they prepare. If their children reject their food, they feel personally rejected and need to force their children to eat everything they put on their plates in order to feel acceptable as parents. Most obese people had parents who insisted they eat every bite on their plates.

There are other misguided parents who play silly games with their children to get them to eat more food than they want or need. They tell their children that, "Santa Claus is watching to see how much you eat," or, "The little elves are looking through the window," or, "God wants you to eat and grow up big and strong." Self-respecting children feel like throwing their food at their parents and reclaiming their own appetites and stomachs, but sit meekly in confusion and unhappiness, and develop emotional blocks to normal enjoyment of food that will follow them the rest of their lives. Obesity, self-starvation, bizarre food preferences, and a host of digestive problems can usually be directly traced to such asinine mealtime traumas in childhood.

If we can somehow get food back into its proper place, as a source of necessary fuel for the body as well as a source of physical and emotional satisfaction, we can probably do a lot to end the plethora of minor discomforts so many children and adults have—not to mention the major problems of hyperactivity and learning disability.

Since we all received our first nourishment while being held and cuddled, we all associate food with love and security.

So it's extremely important to keep mealtime a pleasurable time, with a minimum of lecturing about table manners. However, it's also important for children to learn that mealtime is pleasurable for adults, also, and not a time to show off their belching ability or to kick their brothers under the table. Rather than ruin everybody's meal with lectures and punishment, it's usually more effective to pleasantly observe that the person supplying the unwelcome sound effects or gymnastic feats in the dining chair is probably not hungry and might prefer leaving the table. If he really *is* hungry, he'll get the idea and settle down. If he's not, he shouldn't be forced to eat.

When Baby Fat Doesn't Melt Away

While we're discussing the common problem of parents who try to overfeed their children, let's not forget the parents who are frustrated because they aren't successful in helping their children lose weight. Most children are overweight because they consume more calories than they burn up in activity. Every calorie not spent in activity will be stored in a child's body as fat. An obese child is not only carrying unnecessary fat, but he is setting a pattern of obesity that will almost certainly stay with him throughout his life.

Most professionals who work with obese children aim toward maintaining the children's weight rather than trying to get them to lose the excess. Their rationale is that a child who is four feet tall at ninety pounds will grow, and at five feet the ninety pounds will be appropriate. So an obese child's diet is designed to prevent further weight *gain*, and not to cause a weight loss.

While a nutritionist can design a diet specifically tailored to a child's age, weight, and height, you can't go very far wrong if you stick to a diet designed around moderate amounts of lean meats, fresh fruits and vegetables, whole grain cereals, and limited amounts of eggs and dairy products. It's almost impossible to gain weight on a diet that has no refined flour or sugar in it, so long as other foods are eaten in reasonable amounts.

In very rare instances, a child will continue to gain weight in spite of a minimum caloric intake. If there is no hormonal problem and the child is otherwise healthy, such a contrary pattern of weight gain may be due to a missing enzyme which helps regulate the utilization of food to energy. Dr. Jeffrey Flier and his colleagues at the Boston Beth Israel Hospital are currently engaged in trying to synthesize the enzyme in question so that those unfortunate people who find it impossible to maintain a desired weight through dieting can be rescued by chemical means. Until there is help from the laboratory, however, obese children and adults will have to rely on exercise and minimum calories to maintain good health.

I can't stress enough how extremely important it is for you as a parent to give food a very positive and health-producing place in your child's life. A child's brain has its most crucial stages of growth in the first two years of life, and then continues to develop for several more years. If the necessary nutrients for optimal brain growth are missing during these early years, there will never be another opportunity to make up for lost brain cell growth later, and a child will fail to develop to his full intellectual, social, and emotional potential. So it's vitally important for you to provide the good wholesome food your child needs if he is to develop as well as he possibly can. During these early formative years, it's more important for him to have nutritious food than it is for him to have attractive clothes or fancy toys, so if you must budget carefully, let your child play with homemade toys and wear hand-me-downs, and spend as much of your budget as you can on wholesome food.

Equally important is that the food be presented in a calm and reasonable manner, in an atmosphere of love and acceptance, so that food will be eaten and assimilated in a healthy way. To purchase and prepare nutritious meals and then create an atmosphere that causes a child to lose his appetite or to develop bizarre emotional reactions to food will defeat your original purpose and create problems you don't need to have.

There's no need to make food a religion, but if mealtimes are pleasant, with smiling faces and friendly conversation, and if food is simple and as unprocessed as possible, there will be fewer emotional and learning problems for children and for their parents. There's really no reason why our affluent nation can't provide that basic element in every child's life.

Children begin by loving their parents; as
they grow older they judge them; sometimes
they forgive them.

                              -Oscar Wilde

Chapter Four

STAY CALM, ALL KIDS STEAL

Let me tell you a true story. There once was a little boy, about four years old, who was very loving and affectionate to everyone in his world. He loved to give presents to his parents and to his older brother, and would labor long hours in his room drawing and coloring and cutting and pasting works of art to give to them. One late autumn day when he and his mother were shopping in a department store, they passed a counter filled with gaudy costume jewelry, resplendent with colored glass and fake "diamonds." He was quite entranced, and excitedly pointed out one especially ostentatious broach to his mother, saying, "Look, Mommy! That's *beautiful!*" His mother politely agreed, so as not to hurt his feelings, and hurried him along to another part of the store, secretly marveling at the garishness of the jewelry.

Weeks passed, and the mother completely forgot the display of exquisitely atrocious jewelry until Christmas morning, when she opened a clumsily-wrapped package from her young son. With eyes shining almost as brightly as the colored rhinestones on the broach, he crowed, "I got it for you, Mommy, and you didn't even know it!"

With a terrible sinking feeling, the mother knew that she was the recipient of a piece of hot jewelry, and while her sense of honesty told her she should scold him for "stealing," she realized that he had no idea of any wrong-doing, and her admiration for his ability to hide the broach for several weeks without letting his secret out caused her to feel pride in his ingenuity and self-control. And her recognition of his love and excitement which would be crushed if she rejected his gift caused her heart to melt. With a resolve to go to the store and pay the store manager for the broach, she kissed him soundly, pinned on the broach and wore it proudly all Christmas day. Now, fifteen years later, it still rests in gaudy splendor in its cotton bed in a box in my dressing table drawer.

Discovering that they're harboring a very small thief in their midst usually causes parents to feel anger, guilt, and fear. Parents who would go back to a store to return a penny may find themselves with a youngster who appears to be headed for the penitentiary because of his guiltless pilfering, while parents who may hedge a little on their income taxes or keep silent when given too much change nevertheless find themselves shaken by pint-sized crime.

I remember a mother who told of taking her six-year-old son shopping and noted that he was hiding something under his shirt as they left the department store. Remembering that he had asked for a book in the toy department, she suspiciously asked if he had taken the book. The boy denied that he had, and as soon as they returned home hurriedly went to his room and shut the door. Alarmed, the mother went to his room and told him she would not punish him for taking the book if he told her the truth about it, but that he would surely be punished if he had taken the book and did not admit it. With wide-eyed protestations of innocence, her son declared that he had no book. The mother, feeling like a Gestapo agent, looked under his bed and predictably found the stolen book.

In mounting fury and disgust, she angrily took both the book and the child back to the department store, where she self-righteously made the boy apologize to the clerk and return the book. She drove home in a shaken mood, sternly lecturing the child all the way, and was tremendously relieved when they reached home, where she planned to have a long hot bath and a long cold drink and try to forget the entire incident. To her horror, a stolen toy fell from under his shirt as her son climbed from the car.

"I was too ashamed to go back to the store," she said

ruefully when recalling the incident, "and I was too weak to do anything to him. So I called my husband and cried and told him our son was a thief, and that it was all his fault for being away from home so much. I never saw the toy again, so I suppose he threw it away or lost it. I still don't know how I should have handled it."

Since her son was an honors student in college at the time of the telling, with every indication of being an honest, responsible, conscientious individual, it wasn't any longer necessary for his mother to "handle" the situation in any way. But her embarrassment at something which had taken place almost thirteen years earlier was still acute, and was typical of the feeling of inadequacy and failure that most parents feel in similar situations.

Learning About Ownership

The fact is that almost all children steal something at some time, and most children steal several things several times. It's therefore a normal childhood occurrence, and doesn't indicate a tendency toward future lawlessness. Unless a child is guided to understand that stealing is unacceptable, however, he may indeed never learn to respect the property of others or to understand that stealing is intolerable.

In this, as in all other normal stages of development, parents have to avoid being so open-minded that their brains fall out, while at the same time accepting and understanding the normalcy of the situation. Overreaction may set up feelings of guilt and worthlessness in a child that may cause him to live up to a label of "thief," while underreaction, or avoiding the entire issue, may cause him to assume that his behavior is acceptable, and continue it long past the time when it is appropriate.

To know what constitutes over- or underreaction, you have to understand how a child views taking another's possessions. To a two-year-old, there is no such thing as property that belongs to somebody else, because she firmly believes that everything in the world belongs to *her*. She will scream indignantly if another child holds on to something she wants, regardless if the other child had it first, and she will be totally convinced that *her* rights are being violated if she is denied what she wants. At this age, taking something that belongs to another person is no more stealing than it would be stealing if you saw your rake lying in the backyard and moved it into your garage.

However, while you may sympathize with your toddler when she believes that another child's toys belong to her, you will delay her development if you merely smile and allow her to bully other children. By the same token, you will delay her normal development if you angrily slap her or scream at her or punish her for behaving in a way that is appropriate and normal for a two-year-old.

You can begin teaching her the concept of ownership at this stage by gently but firmly removing the desired toy from her greedy grasp, while saying, "I know you *wish* that toy belonged to you, but it belongs to Michelle." Since she will usually lunge at Michelle to retrieve the toy, you would be wise to scoop her up in your arms as soon as you have returned the toy to Michelle, thereby avoiding the possibility of a tug-of-war, and at the same time saving yourself embarrassment.

Expect some loud protests and some tears, but if you quickly find something to take the place of the desired object, with a repeated, "This belongs to you," you may be successful in preventing a scene, but if not, continue to be firm but gentle, with repeated enumerations of toys that belong to her, and toys that belong to other children. "The wagon belongs to Kimberly, the truck belongs to Jesse, the ball belongs to Amy." Expect frequent episodes such as this, and don't expect the idea of ownership to sink in for a few more years, but continue with your gentle repetitions of who owns what, without allowing yourself to resort to either anger or apathy.

By the time your youngster is around four years old, he will know that other toys *belong* to other children, but he will still feel that they will *belong* to him if they are in his possession. He will be less blatantly aggressive about attempting to gain the things he wants than he was at two, but only because he realizes the adults in his life will prevent his doing so. Thus, a four-year-old may secretly take a toy from another child's yard, and then quite openly play with it in his own yard because he believes that he has obtained ownership of it "fair and square." He will be quite astonished and hurt if adults force him to return the objects to their rightful owner.

Again, it will do no good to become angry or excited. Simply go with him while he returns the toys, telling him, "I know you *wish* that ball belonged to you, but it belongs to Kevin. Perhaps you will get one like it for your birthday, and then you will have a ball that belongs to you."

Since a four-year-old has a hard time distinguishing between wishes and reality—as will be discussed in the chapter on lying—he may reply indignantly, "It *is* mine!" Again, firmly but with good humor, repeat, "You *wish* it was yours."

By the time he is about six, he will know to hide the things he takes from other people, or from stores, and he will most likely deny taking them when confronted. He will continue to be confused and hurt, however, if he is punished for taking things that belong to other people, because he still has a hazy notion of the idea of ownership. He will realize that the adults in his life become disturbed when he brings home things that did not originate there, but he will still not completely understand why he should not be allowed to appropriate for himself things he would like to have.

At this age, he will frequently take things that are small and which fit easily in his pockets. Chalk from school, a tiny doll from a friend's dollhouse, a nickle, a miniature racecar, or similar items may be in his pockets when his jeans reach the laundry, and if asked where the items came from, he is likely to brilliantly respond, "I dunno," or to say, "Erin gave me that," or, "I found it on the sidewalk," or something equally vague. Since he also has a vague idea of the difference between an idea and a memory, he will probably really believe what he says, and will become terribly crushed if you question his truthfulness.

Since you really can't prove where the items originated, and since there is a possibility that he is telling the truth, and since all his friends' parents are probably finding small toys that belong to him in their children's pockets, it's best to give him the benefit of the doubt and keep silent about it. If you find something that you know beyond doubt belongs to the school or to a friend, simply tell him very firmly that he will have to return it, and tell him that it is unfair to other people to take their possessions, and that he would not like for other people to take his things.

By the time a child is about eight, he will usually have stopped taking things that don't belong to him, except for occasional lapses, and he will report another child's stealing with a ferocious self-righteousness born of having so recently been an unrepentant snatcher instead of snitcher. By the time he is around ten, he will have the same values his parents have regarding property rights and ownership if they have given him proper guidance, and he can be expected to conform to his parents' standards.

So how do you provide "proper guidance?" You do so by keeping your sense of humor and your respect for your child as she moves from one developmental stage to another. You do so by gently and firmly repeating a thousand times, "You *wish* that belonged to you. Things belong to you when you buy them in a store or when somebody gives them to you, like on your birthday or at Christmas."

When and if she takes something that belongs to another person, don't make a federal issue of it, and don't say stupid things like, "The police come and put people in jail who steal things," or, "Jesus is crying because you took something that didn't belong to you," or, "The devil in you did that, didn't he?"

Bear in mind that the word "steal" is an abstraction which has absolutely no meaning to a child under the age of six, and even then it is a word which he hears adults using, but whose meaning is unclear. Children attach meanings to words which have reference to things they can see or touch or hear, but abstract concepts have little meaning. The concept of ownership may have to be repeated many times, with concrete examples, before he completely understands it. You can make it clearer by explaining how things become one's property and by offering to help him earn money to buy things he wants, or by helping him prepare a list of things he would like to have as gifts on birthdays and holidays.

Many parents can tolerate their child's appropriating another child's toys with equanimity, but fall apart when they discover change missing from their pocketbook. Money seems to be more sacrosanct than ordinary possessions, and the taking of money frequently prompts parents to abandon hope that their child is worthy of salvation.

If the money-taking culprit is a three- or four-year-old, or even an eight-year-old, don't despair. Make sure you don't leave small change lying carelessly about to tempt a sticky-fingered youngster, and sternly tell him that he is not to touch money in your wallet or purse or in other parts of the house. If the child is over the age of eight, and especially if he is over the age of ten, there is reason for concern, and you would be wise to seriously look at the situation.

Your child may be trying to communicate distress of some sort to you. Perhaps he needs more of your time and attention; perhaps he's feeling insecure regarding the family stability; perhaps he's afraid of losing you. Also, evaluate your own values and practices where money is concerned. Do you chortle when you notice that a supermarket checker has charged you less for an item than the advertised price? Do you laugh in admiration when a television newscaster tells of a bank robber who made a daring heist during the busiest hour? Do you regale your family with stories of how you "conned" a shopowner or a dentist or a florist or a repairman into a "deal" that saved you money? In other words, are you teaching your child to steal and then punishing him for it?

Whether or not you have inadvertantly coached your

youngster in the art of stealing, if he is over the age of ten, he needs help. Compulsive stealing, especially when objects are taken for which the child has no real desire and which may be abandoned once they are stolen, indicates a deep-seated emotional distress which should be promptly attended to.

If you are reasonably happy, well-adjusted, and honest, however, and if you approach the problem of "stealing" in very young children in a matter-of-fact manner, without resorting to moralistic hysterics or to laissez-faire indifference, the chances are remote that your child will ever have a serious problem about stealing.

Humiliation Is A Poor Teacher

Understanding the fact that your child will have no clear concept of ownership until she is about ten years old, and that stealing in young children is age-appropriate behavior doesn't eliminate the problem of what to do when you discover that she has happily filched something from a store. If and when you are confronted with such a problem, you have several alternatives. You can tell her that she is a wicked, awful child and march her back to the store and force her to "confess" her crime to the manager. Or you can insist that she pray to God to forgive her for her sin of thievery. Or you can secretly slip the item back on the store's shelf when the clerks aren't looking, and then go home and have a good cry.

Or you can take the more direct way and say, "You *wish* this was yours to keep, but it isn't. We'll have to take it back. I can't allow you to keep things that don't belong to you. If you'd like to buy it, I'll help you find some jobs around the house and make the money to buy it, and then it'll really be yours."

For heaven's sake, when you return the child and the item to the store, don't make a huge dramatic production out of it by humiliating the child with forced apologies and confessions. A simple, "We want to return this. My daughter took it *by mistake*" is sufficient. Don't be afraid that your child will never learn to respect the ownership of property if you fail to humiliate her when she is caught with things that don't belong to her. The fact is that children want to be cooperative, and they will be sociable, honorable people if they are gently guided in that direction, without stripping them of their self-respect.

Certainly, children should be taught that things belonging to another person cannot be taken away from that person simply because one wants them. And they must be taught that *everything* in a store or in another person's yard or home belongs to *someone* and that it can only be acquired by buying it, by trading something for it, or by receiving it as a gift. If children are never taught this fact, they may very well continue to take whatever they want, without any sense of guilt or of responsibility.

When the lesson of ownership is taught with too much harshness and humiliation, however, the result may be a deep, pervasive feeling of guilt which may persist for life and which may interfere with a child's ability to form mature relationships with other people. Psychotherapists frequently encounter patients in therapy who are the victims of parental training that was aimed at instilling respect for property rights of other people, but was carried out in such a heavyhanded manner that the person feels vaguely guilty all the time.

If a person whose parents were overly punitive in response to childish stealing hears that a neighbor's home has been burglarized, he will immediately wonder if he will be suspected. If he sees a store detective, he will fear that he is suspected of shoplifting. He may live in constant anxiety lest he be accused of a crime, when he may have never stolen anything, and in fact may be scrupulously honest.

Men and women with these vague feelings of guilt and apprehension are almost always victims of parents who instilled a deep sense of guilt in them when they were children, before they developed a clear sense of truth or of ownership. By overreacting to natural childish possessiveness and egocentricity, their parents caused them to feel like criminals for the rest of their lives, thereby destroying their sense of worth as people.

To get an idea of how children feel when they are judged by adult standards before they have acquired a concept of ownership, imagine that you go to visit another country without studying the laws of that country before you arrive there. The people in the other country are unusually large, and tower over you, often speaking in a language which they assume you understand, but which is largely incomprehensible to you.

Imagine that you walk along the street, looking at the sights around you, dodging the large people who dwarf you. As you walk along, you notice that there are brightly colored stones lying on the walk. The stones sparkle and have a translucent quality which intrigues you, and you stoop and pick one up to examine it. It is a particularly beautiful gem of some kind, and you are amazed that they are littering the walk. Feeling pleased to have such a pretty souvenir, you put it in your pocket.

Immediately, several of the giants descend on you, roughly shoving you around and shouting at you. One pulls the stone from your pocket, another slaps you, and several angrily yell charges at you such as, "Don't you know better than to take things that don't belong to you?" or, "You little thief, those stones belong to the King!" or, "You don't deserve to walk on our street, you bad person!"

You no doubt would leave that country as soon as possible, since you would feel very uncomfortable and anxious there and would fear inadvertantly violating another of the unknown laws. If you were unable to leave, however, or if you were not allowed to leave, you would eventually feel extremely frustrated, guilty, and confused at being punished and berated for breaking the law, when you did not know what the law was.

If, however, one of the giants had gently stopped you and said something like, "I see you are a stranger here, and you probably don't know that those stones are the property of the King. We know you wish you could keep one, but we are not allowed to touch them, since the King wants them left in the street for all to enjoy," you would have emptied your pocket, thanked the giant for explaining the law to you, and thenceforth left all colored stones lying in the street. And most important, you would have felt that you were respected, and that you had been corrected but not condemned, and that you had been treated with courtesy as befits a person of worth.

When dealing with children, bear in mind that they are strangers in a world new to them, and the laws and rules of the world must be explained to them before they can obey them. Bear in mind, too, that children think in idiosyncratic ways, and that words which mean one thing to us may mean something entirely different to them. They may have to have rules explained to them many times before they can understand them and incorporate them into their own thinking. They will understand more readily and they will have far more respect for themselves and for other people if rules are explained to them in a gentle, objective manner. To treat children as if they are criminals does not teach them to respect the rights of others, it simply teaches them to feel guilty.

When Stealing Is And Isn't Normal

The most appropriate way to deal with your child's "stealing," then, depends on his age and the particular situation. If he is ten or over, he may have significant inner conflicts which need professional attention. His stealing may reflect feelings of inadequacy or inferiority which cause him to need to steal to gain attention or a feeling of power. He may also steal because he has somehow been taught to steal, either at home or by other influences.

If your child is eight, and only occasionally has a rare episode of taking something that does not belong to her, the stealing probably indicates lapses into more immature feelings. In her case, you probably would be wise to sit down with her and remind her that everyone has the right to keep his or her possessions. There probably should be some appropriate punishment for stealing at this age—a night without TV, forfeiting a week's allowance to repay money taken, or some such reminder—but don't resort to endless lectures or sermonizing. The realization that you are displeased is usually enough to cause an eight-year-old to end her stealing career. If your eight-year-old frequently and compulsively steals, she needs help to resolve whatever underlying conflicts she has.

At six, stealing may be furtive and planned one time, and open and spontaneous the next. If you frequent a drive-in grocery or a supermarket where you pay the clerk for a carton of soft drinks which you then pick up on the way out the door, your six-year-old may very likely pick up a carton of soft drinks one day and walk out without paying, proudly emulating you with a total lack of awareness that he is "stealing."

At his age, a reminder that one pays for items in a store and that *you* always have paid for the drinks before you pick them up is usually sufficient. Explain that storeowners pay for the goods they sell and that they have to collect money from other people for them. Rather than embarrass him in front of the store clerk by exposing his ignorance, go back with him to the clerk, loyally hold his hand and say, "We forgot to pay for these drinks." Your child will thereby learn several things: that you are loyal to him and sensitive to his feelings; that you are honorable and fair; and that soft drinks have to be paid for.

A four-year-old is a different matter. A four-year-old lives in never-never land, where facts are whatever one wishes them to be and where possession determines ownership. A four-year-old is also extremely sensitive, and her feelings are easily hurt. To a four-year-old who has "stolen" something, very earnestly and honestly say, "I'm sorry, I can't let you keep it. It belongs to Andy, and he wants to keep it."

When she protests that she also wants to keep it, tell her firmly that she can't keep it because it isn't her's. Remind her of how she got her favorite doll, her building blocks, her treasured teddy bear, and help her imagine how she would feel if another child took her possessions.

Keep your sense of humor and don't be concerned if your conversations end with an avowed determination on her part to regain the toy you've made her return to its rightful owner. It's at moments like these that you will hear faintly in your memory the voice of your mother saying, "I only hope that you will have a child as stubborn as you!"

The two-year-old, of course, simply reacts to his feelings and to the things around him, and if you try to talk about "owning" things, or "stealing" things, you're wasting your breath.

At all ages, in all things, try to steer a course between the Scylla of indifference and the Charybdis of catastrophizing. Try not to look on childish appropriation of others' things as "stealing" in the adult sense of the word, and try to see it as a child's egocentric method of experiencing the world.

Also, remember that such egocentricity is right and appropriate for a child, and that while the idea that "whatever exists, exists for me" is not appropriate in an adult, it is not only appropriate but necessary for a child. As he grows and matures, he will gradually become aware of other people and of their rights and become cooperative and responsible in dealing with them.

Don't make the common mistake of believing that children are just short people who think and feel like tall people. Children think and reason in totally different ways than adults do, and in order to guide them to mature understanding, you have to see life from their point of view and understand how they operate. Otherwise, you'll sow seeds of discord when they're very small that you'll ruefully reap when they're very tall—maybe taller than you.

We must make the world
honest before we can honestly
say to our children that
honesty is the best policy.
    -George Bernard Shaw

Chapter Five

I HATE TO TELL YOU, BUT ALL KIDS LIE, TOO

You say that your child not only steals, but he also lies? If you ask him a direct question about who left the gate unlocked so the dog got out, does he suggest that perhaps the dog did? Does he come home from school and tell you tall tales about a band of gypsies who tried to steal him and how he single-handedly fought the gypsy leader who had long black hair and one gold earring? Does he tell you that he made an A in Math, and then you see his report card and discover that he made a D? Does he tell you that his grades are low because his teacher hates him and picks on him and then you discover that he never turns in homework? Are you losing respect for him, and do you believe that he is a pathological liar?

If the answer to the first two questions is yes, then you are a fairly normal parent with a fairly normal child. But if your answer is yes to the other questions, you may have a problem, especially if he is more than ten or eleven years old. As in all other aspects of childish behavior, the measure of whether or not lying is cause for alarm depends on the age of the child and the circumstances surrounding the lie.

To understand childish untruths, one must understand and remember the normal developmental stages of childhood, which move from a purely egocentric stage to a social, cooperative stage. The developmental stages can't and shouldn't be altered or accelerated, because each is important to a child in establishing a healthy identity and relationship with the world. It's difficult for adults to imagine what a purely egocentric framework is, in which whatever one believes *is*, and whatever one thinks of is experienced as a memory, and in which the world and everything in it revolves around oneself. But that's how an infant experiences himself and the world, and the time from infancy through adolescence is a slowly evolving process of discarding one bit of egocentricity after another. It's not a parent's job to change that process, but to facilitate it and to try to prevent a child from "freezing" in one stage of development and not moving onward.

All of us know adults who never outgrew some of the egocentric stages, who are selfish, self-centered, demanding, and who lie pathologically with seeming disregard for the patent transparency of their lies. These are people who don't choose to be immature, but who are behaving in ways that are appropriate to children but inappropriate for adults. They simply never grew up.

Guiding Them Toward Honesty

You can help your own children grow up by being mature enough yourself to accept the appropriateness of childlike behavior. You also have to be mature enough to gently guide your children toward adult behavior without forcing it upon them too soon or too harshly. You must not expect your children to come into the world with a full set of adult standards regarding truth any more than you expect them to be born with a full set of permanent teeth.

A child who is harshly punished for behaving in a way that is appropriate for his stage of development may never acquire a mature concept of truth, but be frozen at an immature level of viewing truthfulness as merely something that other people demand and not as a medium of cooperation between people. On the other hand, children who are given no guidance toward truthfulness may never acquire a mature concept of truth or may have to learn it painfully from the outside world.

Parents often become alarmed or bemused when their toddler utters his first "lie," not realizing that this is a healthy indication that their child has mastered the process of individuation from his mother. From infancy until shortly after a child gains speech, he will not be able to distinguish himself apart from his mother. He is sure that his mother knows his thoughts and feels his feelings.

At some point, he becomes aware that he exists separately from his mother, that he is an individual in his own right. It is at this point, needing to test his new selfhood and to affirm it to himself, that a healthy child will utter his first "lie" or perform his first act of "disobedience." Usually these first verbalized indicators of individuation are in the form of the word "No!" uttered loudly and firmly and often irrationally.

Offer a toddler who is filled with the heady sense of individuation a favorite toy and he will refuse it, saying "No!" Ask him if he made the puddle on the floor, and he will stand with dripping pants and glaringly retort, "No!" Ask him if he wants to go for a ride, and he will defiantly say, "No!" while heading for the car. Don't despair, and don't fear that you've beget a contrary monster. Your child is simply discovering the fact that he's separate from you.

When children are two or three years old, they believe unquestioningly every thought which enters their heads, and experience their thoughts as memories. Until they are about four, they believe everything they tell. Thus, a child of this age can look at a picture of a horse and say, "That's my horse," or, "That's my Daddy's horse," and while he is making the statement, there is no doubt in his mind that the horse is indeed his or his father's, even though he may have only seen a horse at a distance once or twice in his lifetime.

A child's mind at this age is easily triggered into idea-memories, which he will firmly believe and defend. An example of this was a converstation between Danny, a four-year-old friend of mine, and Angie, his seven-year-old neighbor who had just returned from a trip to Disneyland.

72

"I rode in a boat," Angie told a group of children, "and there were alligators in the water!"

"I went to Disneyland yesterday," interjected Danny eargerly. "I rode in a boat too, and an alligator bit the boat and made a hole in it and the water camed in!"

His older companions turned on him in disgust and exclaimed, "You did not! You're lying!"

"I am not!" wailed Danny. "I did too go! Yesterday! With my Daddy!"

And while his disdainful playmates, whose own concept of truth was none too firm, continued to taunt him for such an obvious untruth, he remained self-righteously indignant that they did not believe him.

By an adult's standards, Danny was lying. But by a young child's standards, one verbal account of an experience has as much validity as another, and his trip to Disneyland was therefore as real and truthful as was his neighbor's, since he couldn't actually see or feel either trip.

Very young children have great difficulty distinguishing their own realities from that of others. If you tell your youngster about something you did when you were small, she is quite likely to reply, "I was with you when you did that."

She is not lying or teasing or being silly. The experience became real to her when she heard about it, and it seems to her that she remembers it, even though she just heard about it. Since young children can't imagine a time when they weren't, and since they will experience other people's accounts of happenings as their own memories, it will only be logical for them to assume that they were also present when their parents were children.

Only when children have developed a stronger sense of identity and of being separate from everyone else will they experience their lives as separate from the lives of their parents. Then they will realize that their experiences happen to them and to nobody else, and that other people have experiences which happen only to them.

Sometime around the age of five or six, children gradually become aware that they sometimes say things that displease their adults, but the concept of lying is alien to them, and the words "lie" or "truth," being abstract concepts, have absolutely no meaning to them. Many small children believe that a "lie" is a naughty word, since they may be punished for "telling a lie" and for saying a "naughty word." Since they have no comprehension of what either a lie or a naughty word is, but know that each is something that comes from their mouths, they conclude that a lie and a naughty word is the same thing.

Parents usually fail to understand the inability of small children to comprehend the meaning of abstract words, and believe they're being understood when they demand, "Now you tell me the *truth!*" A child may solemnly nod and promise to tell the truth, or assert that whatever he has just told is the truth, but the fact is that children haven't the foggiest notion what "truth" actually means, since something is *true* because you say it is.

It's for this reason that you should be extremely cautious in questioning young children when their answers are to be used as evidence for or against another child or adult. More than one older child or adult has been unfairly accused of sexual misconduct with a child because an adult who didn't understand how a child's mind works has become alarmed and planted ideamemories in a child's mind by the manner in which they asked questions.

If you ask a child, "Tell me what happened," and you hear a graphic description of fondling or exposure of genitals, the account is probably factual. However, if you ask, "Did he...?" or "Did you...?" you're likely to get a "Yes" answer simply because when you presented the idea it became transformed into a "memory." And the child will be solemnly confident that he or she is telling the "truth."

All young children express their wishes or hopes or fears as if they were factual. This is partly because they haven't the vocabulary to say, "I wish I could..." or "I'm afraid that..." and partly because all the impressions which float across their minds have equal reality. A memory of a dog actually seen and the idea of a dog somebody talks about and the wish for a dog of his own are all equally real to a young child, so that he may tell a stranger all about his nonexistent dog, describing in detail its color, name, size, and age. Since it only exists at the moment he tells about it, he isn't surprised to find it absent when he goes home, but if the stranger accompanies him, he may be surprised and disconcerted at his own belief in what the child said.

By the age of five, most children are dimly aware that there is a difference between concrete reality and what they wish to be true, but they will still express wishes as if they were facts. This is part of a child's magical thinking, which expects wishes to become concrete reality, and the expectation becomes momentarily translated into belief.

Young children will also express their fears as facts. It is for this reason that children's dreams are so confusing, since what happens while they are sleeping is as real as what happens while they are awake. In dealing with the patent untruths uttered by children under the age of seven or eight, you must remember that children may be expressing their feelings, wishes, or fears when they tell stories or give explanations, and that they are not always expressing beliefs.

Even when parents realize the difference between a lie and a child's manner of expressing his egocentric thoughts, they may still feel vaguely uncomfortable at simply accepting untruths as if they believed them. Not wanting to hurt a child's feelings by saying, "I don't believe that," or to damage her esteem by saying, "You're just fibbing," parents may smile in tight-lipped discomfort as their small child prattles on about how she just flew in on the wings of a large bird and landed in the back yard. Eventually, the parents may become so uncomfortable they'll say something like, "That's just pretend, isn't it?"

Since their child will have as little understanding of the word "pretend" as she has of "lie" or "truth", she will agree because it seems to be what her parents want her to do. Her parents may feel more comfortable, and the child certainly isn't damaged by being exposed to the word "pretend," but she isn't any closer to understanding truthfulness, either.

It's more effective to restate what the child is saying in a way that she will understand, without commenting on the words she is using to communicate her meaning. For example, if you say, "It would be fun to fly on top of a bird," you will acknowledge the fact that she is using her imagination in an entertaining way.

On the other hand, if she seems to be communicating alarm, your correct response would be, "Some birds *seem* big enough to pick you up and fly away with you, but they really can't. Birds can't carry people."

Your response is not saying, "I don't believe you," but, "I understand that you are telling me something you fear might happen," and a child will accept your reassurance for what it is.

If you continue to interpret "lies" and verbally reflect back to your child the wishes or fears the lies represent, you will help her learn to sort out fact from fantasy, the first step in acquiring a mature concept of truth.

For example, five-year-old Josh gazed at his new next-door neighbor, a tolerant gentleman with several grandchildren, and announced, "I'm in the third grade."

His new friend grinned at Josh and said, "You *wish* you were in the third grade. You would *like* to be in the third grade."

Josh grinned back and said, "I *am* in the third grade," and a friendship based on understanding and acceptance began. The neighbor understood that Josh was expressing wishes and not deceitful untruths. Josh understood that his neighbor accepted his statements as legitimate *feelings* and felt accepted and respected. To have responded in the way that adults usually do, with confrontations or denials or accusations, would have confused Josh and would not have made him any more honest.

Somewhere around the age of six, children begin to

define a lie as something that is not true, but they judge a lie as any incorrect statement, whether or not the statement is meant to deceive. A six-year-old will likely believe his mother has "lied" to him, for example, if she makes him wear a raincoat to school because she believes it's going to rain and it doesn't.

Around this age, children believe a lie that is punished is much more serious than one that isn't. If the punishment was very severe, the child will believe the lie was a very bad one. At this age, children make a conscious effort to stick to the facts, but only because they are aware their adults expect them to do so and that they will be punished for telling untruths.

Thus, they begin to feel a responsibility for telling the truth to adults—not because they believe telling an untruth is morally wrong, but because it is considered wrong by adults. They still have no understanding of why lies are forbidden, but they want to please their adults and avoid punishment, so they become aware of the need to stick to what is real.

Curiously, six-year-olds frequently regress in the area of truthfulness, and while they are aware of the need for fact-related verbalizations, they may become totally irrational when caught in a forbidden act, and flatly deny any responsibility even when the evidence is overwhelming. If they are accused of lying, they usually become very emotional and distraught.

This is probably because a six-year-old has so many pressures coming at him from all directions that he can't cope with all of them and has to revert a bit to a more immature stage. At a time when he is being thrust out into the world of classrooms and teachers, expected to learn to read and to sit still and listen and to stand in line to go to the bathroom and to give up all infantile pleasures, it may be simply too much to expect a six-year-old to also move on to absolute truthfulness. Parents need to be a little more tolerant of a six-year-old's emotional disequilibrium and allow him a little leeway in the area of truthfulness. So if your six-year-old tells you that a big brown bear comes into the yard each night and looks through his bedroom window, accept it as an expression of his anxiety and need for a little extra cuddling and security, and don't accuse him of lying to you.

A child of seven or eight is usually fairly truthful, and is almost always extremely concerned with other people's truthfulness. An eight-year-old will be quick to accuse her classmates of lying but she may still sometimes express her own feelings in the form of untruths, since her primary interest is still to please her parents and teachers, and since she still finds it difficult to comprehend the exact nature of a lie.

An eight-year-old may tell lies in a teasing manner in order to demonstrate her knowledge of truthfulness, and also to test her adults' ability to detect a falsehood. Eight-year-olds are usually fairly honest about confessing misdeeds, however, and are beginning to understand that truth is necessary in order to know what to expect from other people.

By the time children are about nine years old, they are almost completely honest, but they still relate honesty to the people who are most important to them. Your nine-year-old, for example, may lie to her peers in order to feel important, but she will usually be honest with you, unless you encourage lying by the way you handle questions and punishment.

For example, you encourage lying if you ask, "Have you been eating cookies?" when you see the cookie jar moved to the front of the kitchen counter, with a tell-tale trail of cookie crumbs around it and on the floor, and there is only one child in the house. Most red-blooded American children will hope they can escape punishment by lying and will say, "No."

It's not fair to ask a question you already know the answer to and then be angry if you are lied to. Avoid offering the opportunity to lie, and simply state the facts. "You've been eating cookies when the rule is no cookies before dinner. Come clean up the crumbs you left."

Look at it this way: If you went through a traffic light just as it was turning red, and a police officer stopped you and asked, "Did you run that red light?" wouldn't you be tempted to say, "No"? You might very well tell the truth, but if you're like most of us, there would be at least a fleeting moment of temptation, especially if you thought there was a chance he might believe you. You've had a lot more years to develop automatic habits of truthfulness than your child has, so don't test his recently-acquired sense of honesty by giving him an option of lying.

It's also a mistake and a lesson in futility and frustration to try to identify a guilty party when there is room for doubt. If there is more than one child in the house when you discover the cookie jar caper, for example, and nobody has crumbs around his or her mouth, you'll only become frustrated if you demand, "Who's been in the cookies?"

Do you really expect the guilty one to stand up like George Washington and say, "I cannot tell a lie. It was I"? I'm not so sure I believe that even George Washington was that truthful, and I know I don't believe very many children of today or yesterday would immediately confess to such an open question.

You are far more likley to hear a chorus of *Not me's* than you are to hear confessions, and if you press the point, you will likely get a circus of cross-accusations and cross-denials. You would be better off to simply insist that all the possible culprits come and help clean up the crumbs, whether or not they are guilty. You will be accused of being unfair, a child abuser, and un-American, but at least you will be in control of the situation and won't feel the need to catch the next plane to Rio because you can't force your guilty child to confess.

Somewhere around ten or eleven, children begin to understand the full concept of honesty as a basis of mutual trust between people. At this age, children have become fairly well socialized and less egocentric and can distinguish their own or another's mistaken beliefs from lies, as well as their own wishes or fears from facts. From this stage on, children who lie will do so for the same reason adults lie—out of fear or insecurity or a desire to deceive or to protect themselves from real harm.

All children move from a purely egocentric stage of development in which they believe anything they think of and in which they express fears, wishes, or dreams in the form of verbal beliefs, to a stage in which they fully comprehend the reason behind society's need for truthfulness between people or nations. Parents can help guide their children toward truthfulness by simply using some common sense and by trusting the social developmental process just as they trust the physical developmental process.

Stay Grown Up When Your Children Are Childish

Parents rarely fear that their children will fail to grow in stature normally, and they usually trust that their children will develop mature sexual characteristics at the proper time. But they often have little faith in the normal progression toward social maturity in their children—perhaps because they are aware of their own involvement in it. The more socially mature parents are, the more faith they have in their children's future maturity, and the more good-humored they are about the entire process.

If you become too hung up on teaching your children to be scrupulously honest before they have reached a stage at which they can comprehend honesty, you may be stuck in some immature stage of your own development, and do more harm than good to your children.

If there is a memory in your past of a parent screaming in anger at you, "Don't you lie to me!" and if you feel uncomfortable when you must give an explanation to a child's teacher or to some person in authority in your life, wondering if they will believe you, you may have some unresolved conflicts in yourself that need attention, and you're probably creating problems in your children. Many adults expect to meet with distrust and suspicion, no matter how honest they actually are, because their parents were too harsh and too premature in their punishment for dishonesty. They are apt to do to their children what was done to them, and pass along their own sense of uneasiness.

If you find yourself arguing angrily with your preschooler over the accuracy of his statements, your own sense of self-esteem is questionable, and you may need to examine your need to prove your point to somebody who has lived approximately one-tenth of your lifetime.

For example, if your youngster tells you that he has taken a bath, and he obviously is as dusty as he was when he entered the bathroom, do you feel a need to punish him for his lie? Or do you feel comfortable with his childishness, kiss his sticky cheek, tell him, "You *wish* you had already taken a bath, but you haven't yet. Come on, I'll help you find your bathtub toys," and lead him back to the tub?

Are you really concerned with your child's truthfulness, or do you have a secret fear that he is trying to make a fool of you? And if you fear that your youngster will feel he has "won" in an argument over the truthfulness of some inconsequential statement of his, ask yourself why you got into the argument in the first place. Why do you need to "win" an argument with a child? Are you possibly still trying to "win" acceptance from your own parents-in-your-head?

A measure of parents' maturity is usually the amount of equanimity they display when their children behave with age-appropriate egocentricity. If you severely punish your five-year-old for denying that he stepped in a water puddle when his shoes are obviously soaking wet, for example, his behavior is appropriate, while yours is immature.

On the other hand, if you accept his denial as fact, you may encourage him to maintain egocentric behavior long after it is age-appropriate. A mature and helpful response on your part would be, "You *wish* you hadn't stepped in the water, and *I* wish you hadn't stepped in the water, but your shoes are wet and you'd better take them off and dry your feet."

Avoid accusations and guilt-inducing statements such as, "We both know you're lying," or, "Obviously you're not telling the truth." He will understand the concrete reality of wet feet but the abstract concept of lying or truth will be confusing to him and will simply make him anxious.

If the child with the wet feet and the denials of stepping in water is ten years old, on the other hand, it's a mistake to handle his obvious falsehood as if it's an age-appropriate expression of what he wishes were true. If he's ten and intellectually normal and telling such a patent lie, examine the environment in which he lives. Do you mete out such severe punishment that he lies in a desperate hope to escape? Are you somehow encouraging him to lie by stupid questions such as, "Did you step in water?" when he obviously did? Is he so afraid of losing your love or approval that he feels he needs to be perfect at all times and will lie rather than admit imperfection?

Lying About School Grades

Lies told by a child over the age of ten usually are associated with schoolwork or achievement. Generally speaking, a child of this age who lies is trying to make himself appear more competent or more important, or is trying to avoid the responsibility for his schoolwork. So if your child lies and says he made an A when in fact the grade was considerably lower, it may mean that he is afraid you will love him less for not making an A.

If you overemphasize the importance of grades, and in fact gain some of *your* feeling of importance through your child's achievements, you will unwittingly set the stage for possible lying on your child's part. The solution here is for you to find your own areas of achievement, and not attempt to achieve through your children. Every child wants to succeed, but his success should belong to him alone, and not be shared with parents who want to vicariously live through their children.

Be sure that you are not praising and accepting your child only when he accomplishes something. If you do, your child will get the impression that he is valuable to you only for what he accomplishes, and his accomplishments will then belong to you and not to him. Every child needs to feel that he is acceptable and valuable for himself alone, and not for what he accomplishes or achieves. If he is only acceptable or loved when he is achieving success, he will be tempted to lie when he has failed or has not achieved total success, just to forestall the day when you will reject him as a failure.

Paradoxically, parents may create failure in their children when they overemphasize success. A child may be so sure that he can't attain his parents' expectations that he simply won't try. He will fail to do homework because he will be sure it will be below his parents' standards, and then lie and say he lost it because he'll be ashamed to admit to his teacher that he didn't do it. His fear of failure will cause him to become so anxious that he will forget what he knows when taking exams, and then his humiliation at failing will cause him to accuse his teacher of failing to teach the material or of giving ambiguous questions. He may also lie about his grade, hoping for a miracle that will keep his parents from ever discovering the truth.

Sometimes, a child who fears failure will pretend ignorance or indifference, in the belief that it is better to be branded stupid or lazy than to have parents and teachers know that he tried and failed. As in all things, moderation between too much and too little emphasis on achievement in school is the ideal. If you totally ignore a child's grades, neither praising nor punishing, he will have little incentive to achieve success. If you allow him to ignore homework assignments, or to avoid learning new material, and then act as if you believe his lies about how his teacher hates him and gives him bad grades, you're failing on several counts as a parent.

To best help a child feel important and accepted without making him feel a need to lie, praise his passing grades, and especially praise those grades which have improved from his last report card. If he brings a D up to a C, for example, celebrate and congratulate him for a job well done. Don't say, "Now, next time I'll bet you can bring that up to a B!" Zip your lip about what he might do if he "really tried," and concentrate on the present achievement.

If he goes from a C to a D, sympathize with him. Tell him you're sure he feels bad about it. Ask him if there's any trouble you might help with. Does he need more quiet time to study? Does he need you to keep his smaller brothers and sisters away from him while he does his homework? Is he so far behind in the class that he needs a tutor? Can he see the blackboard from where he sits? Can he hear everything the teacher says? Would he like you to help him with memorizing things?

Let him know by your sympathy and concern that you find the grade below your expectations, but that you are not condemning him for it. Offer your help, not your punishment. Discuss the grade with his teacher so that your child knows you are concerned, but don't allow him to feel that you are angry at him for the grade.

In some cases, you may discover that a low grade in a subject is really the best your child can do. If a child is generally competent in most subjects, but has inordinate difficulty in one or two, he may simply have a mental block against learning the material, or he may actually have a specific learning disability. Some very bright youngsters have great difficulty learning foreign languages, for example, and simply are unable to master the sounds or their meanings, no matter how diligently they may try. Others, like Picasso, may be unable to learn the sequence of the alphabet or to learn math adequately.

If your child is making an earnest effort, if his teacher is proficient in teaching the material, if you provide all the help you and he believe is necessary to make it easier to learn, and he still does poorly, accept it. Encourage him to do his best, and tell him this may just not be his year to learn that particular subject. We can't all be proficient in all subjects, and if you demand excellence in all areas, you will not only cause your child great anxiety, but probably lead him to lie or cheat as well.

Lying To Gain Importance

It is your responsibility as a parent to teach your child appropriate table manners, appropriate dress habits, appropriate social responses, et cetera, but you must allow for some childish trial-and-error learning as you go. If you are too harshly critical of your child, you will cause her to feel insignificant and unimportant, and she may then lie to peers in order to feel more important.

A chubby, awkward child who is constantly nagged by her mother for overeating, breaking dishes, tripping over furniture, and tearing her clothes, for example, may make up some fantasy about a trip to Europe with her wealthy grandmother, who introduced her to the Queen. She may embellish her story with descriptions of the palace and tell her classmates how the Queen invited her to visit again next summer.

In a child over the age of ten, this kind of lying is not so much pathological as it is self-defeating. When the other children discover that she has lied to them, they are apt to reject her and call her a liar, thereby creating an even greater sense of insecurity and incompetence.

Every child needs to feel important, and if you find that your child is lying to classmates about personal accomplishments, family wealth, family social position, or the like, the lies are danger signals and should be dealt with promptly. Avoid accusing or condemning, but explore with her in a sympathetic and loving way the reasons for her need to lie to gain a feeling of self-worth. No child should be berated for needing or seeking attention. Instead, she should be helped to find an appropriate manner of gaining attention.

She may not be a first-rate student, for example, but she may excel as a swimmer or gymnast. Or she may be a mediocre student and athlete, but be valued for her even disposition and friendliness. None of us is perfect, and if you find your child lying in an attempt to appear perfect, examine your own attitudes and make sure you haven't created feelings of inadequacy and incompetency that have made her need to bolster her self-esteem.

If you can't find the reason for lying in a child over the age of ten or eleven, get some professional help and don't be surprised if you learn something about yourself as you seek help for your child. In all cases, lying in a child over the age of ten indicates a need, and the need should be the focal point rather than the lie itself. While a child should be aware that a lie is not to be tolerated, he should be helped in finding an appropriate manner of gaining acceptance, importance, and feelings of self-worth, rather than being condemned as a liar.

Are You Teaching Them To Lie?

I don't suppose it needs to be said that you can't expect your child to be any more honest than you are. If you habitually lie to people—even if you believe your lies are "little white lies" that aren't important—you're teaching your child to lie as surely as if you gave him lying lessons. And, worse yet, if you instruct your child to lie for you, don't expect him to believe you when you say you value honesty.

While it's tempting to ask a child to answer the phone and say you're not home when you want to escape a pest, you can expect him to remind you of it when you reprimand him for telling a lie of his own. And if you force your child to protect you from bill collectors or unwelcome neighbors or door-to-door salespeople by answering the door and lying that you're not at home, you will do even more damage to him by adding the need to *appear* honest while lying.

If you demand truthfulness from your children, be sure you are truthful yourself. And if you expect tomorrow's leaders to be honest, be sure you demand honesty in government now. The example you set for your children, and the manner in which you lead them toward mature honesty, may not only affect your family but the entire future of the world.

Sometimes Being Able To Lie Shows Emotional Health

Having said all these admiring words about the virtue of honesty, and how one can help children acquire honesty, I feel compelled to add a short note in defense of appropriate *dis*honesty. There are times when the ability to lie is a sign of healthy emotional adjustment. The person who is totally incapable of lying is too vulnerable and too easily controlled and manipulated by unscrupulous people.

I don't mean that lying to deceive or to cheat or to avoid responsibility indicates emotional maturity. To the contrary, it usually indicates immaturity. But to be able to lie as a means of self-protection is a necessary tool in any well-adjusted person's life.

To illustrate with a fantasy that is totally farfetched and beyond anything you'll ever experience, suppose there were wicked people who wanted to kidnap one of your children. Suppose you hid him in a secret closet which was cleverly concealed and which you were sure the kidnappers would never find.

Now suppose they broke into your home and demanded that you tell them where your child was. If you were unable to completely separate yourself from them, you would feel a horrible sense of helplessness, a certainty that they could see into your mind and know all that was hidden there, and you would passively point out your child's hiding place. If you felt more autonomous, but had feelings of guilt for being untruthful, you might glance quickly in the direction of the hidden closet, thereby giving the kidnappers a nonverbal clue and betraying your child.

If you felt totally autonomous and confident of your ability to use truth or untruth in a responsible, socially appropriate manner without reference to some rule or dogma laid down by some former authority, you would look the kidnappers in the eye and tell them your child had been taken away to a safe place.

Obviously, no parent believes he or she would be so

stupid or weak as to betray his or her own child's safety by feeling compelled to tell the truth in such a bizarre situation. Yet, parents sometimes so zealously go about instilling reverence for the "law" of truth and honesty in themselves and their children that they forget the "spirit" of truth's intent and create helplessness and paralyzed vulnerability in children who can *never* lie, even for their own self-protection. How many children–or adults, for that matter–would instinctively lie or avoid the question posed by a stranger on the telephone regarding the number of people who were home during the day? Most people are so conditioned to tell the truth that they blurt out a factual answer without thinking, and then spend some anxious days wondering if their home is being burglarized while they are away.

While it is probably preferable to be too honest rather than too distrustful and self-defended, it is important to teach children the fact that truth is important as a basis of trust between people of good will, but that there are times when lying or evading the truth is appropriate and necessary when it involves protecting themselves, their homes, or their families from harm.

This distinction between honesty and necessary dishonesty is more important for children past the age of ten or eleven than it is for the very young, since the very young don't understand either concept. Don't fear that cautioning your past-ten-year-old against truthfully answering questions posed by strangers about his home or family will cause him to believe that you have double standards regarding honesty. In fact, most children are pleased to be included in such an adult matter, and readily understand the difference between loose tongues and truthfulness.

Basically, the best advice I can give you regarding honesty in your children is the same that I would give you about almost everything else. Relax, trust them, keep your sense of humor intact, and gently but firmly guide them toward the same standards of truthfulness that you have. If you find that you're overly angry or overly worried or overly defensive when it comes to your child's concept of truth, you may need to examine your anxiety surrounding honesty. You may very well be carrying around unnecessary feelings of guilt or apprehension or anxiety which were transmitted to you by your parents. If so, you will help your child most by ridding yourself of your guilt and anxiety and accepting yourself as you probably are–an honest, caring person who is trusted and valued by other people.

The fault no child ever loses
is the one he was most punished for.
-Casare Beccaria
(1738-1794)

Chapter Six

DON'T GET EXCITED, BUT YOUR KIDS PROBABLY CHEAT

Let's just go ahead and say this and get it over with, since you've probably already guessed. All children cheat at games. Very small children cheat with cheerful abandon, using game pieces or equipment for their own amusement, and, like drunks at a formal banquet, are totally oblivious to any form or procedure followed by other people.

Slightly older children become aware that adults play by "rules," but they don't fully understand what a "rule" is. They believe that one person's rules are as good as another's, so they make their own as they go along.

By the time they reach school age, children become caught up in the concept of winning—although they aren't really sure what "winning" means either. They will copy what they believe other people do in following "rules," and then triumphantly say, "I won!" They seem to feel that "winning" is a matter of making an announcement, and it confuses them if somebody questions how they "won."

Grown up people cheat in order to keep their competitors from winning, since by adult standards there can only be one winner. Children, however, "cheat" in order to win, but they're quite generously willing to allow other players to win also. Furthermore, we can't really call it "cheating" when a child fails to follow game rules and regulations, since he never adopted them for himself in the first place.

From a child's standpoint, your choice to follow certain prescribed game procedures is okay with him. But he expects the same tolerance from you of the way *he* chooses to play. And he sees no reason why your method and his can't be played at the same time, side by side, each enjoying the other's company but not interfering with each other's play. A child of nine or ten has usually mastered the concept of rules and understands that games are meaningless unless all players observe the same rules and abide by them. It is only after this stage that childish ways of playing games can be called "cheating." Even then, a laspe of rule-following may be more a sign of regression into recently outgrown immature behavior than it is of cheating in the adult sense of the word.

An anxious or immature child will continue to cheat past the age of nine or ten, but he will not have the same thrill at winning as a younger child does who doesn't understand the concept of rules. Cheating in a child who understands the concepts of rules may be a symptom of deep insecurity and a fear of growing up and dealing with adult responsibilities. If it persists, or if there is extreme distress at losing a game, it indicates too much concern with winning and an inability to play for the fun of playing. If you find your child of this age persistently and compulsively cheating, ask yourself these questions: Are you communicating a competitive spirit to him? Does he believe he is a loser if he loses? If you play with him, are you ruthless in winning and humiliating in your victory? If so, scale down your own need to win over a child and let him be the child for a change.

Learning To Follow Rules

Like the abstract concept of "truth" or "ownership," the basic concept of "rules" or "laws" is difficult for children to grasp. And just as children move from egocentric thinking to mature understanding of the nature of truth and ownership, so do they move from an egocentric stage in which they can play happily alongside one another, with no regard for the idea of cooperating with one another and sharing a game, to a stage of maturity in which they understand that rules are formed by mutual consent of the people who use them. With total maturity comes the ability to change rules by mutual consent, along with the internalization of those rules which exist for the greater good of all mankind.

Just as a person can become frozen in a particular developmental stage and never progress beyond self-centered, magical thinking, so can he become "stuck" in his understanding of the reasons for rules and laws in his life. If you observe drivers approaching a stop sign for awhile, for instance, you will be able to fairly accurately gauge their various stages of maturity.

The very immature driver runs the stop sign in an egocentric belief that he is a law unto himself, like a two-year-old who believes that everything exists for him. A slightly more mature driver will slow down in a token observance of the sign's intent, because he sees other people stopping, but will continue without a real break in his progress and without allowing other drivers an opportunity to move in an orderly alternate flow.

The driver with a modicum of maturity will stop at the sign, but will fume angrily as if the sign is a living authority put there to slow him down and cause him annoyance. As soon as possible, he will gun his motor and "burn rubber" to show his resentment toward the sign.

The driver frozen in the compulsive rules-keeping stage, but without mature understanding of the purpose of the rules, will anxiously sit at the sign while drivers behind him honk in impatience. This driver can't decide if he has permission from the sign to proceed.

The mature driver, with a clear understanding that the stop sign has been placed at a point where traffic needs to be regulated to allow for safe and orderly cross-flow, will stop to allow the cars in the cross lanes to safely pass, and then will proceed smoothly onward, not lingering longer than necessary nor feeling impatience or anger at the momentary delay.

All rules, whether they are traffic rules, game rules, school rules, or job rules exist for the same purpose. They achieve a degree of orderliness or regularity which allows for a smoothly operating society. To be sure, there are some rules which exist long after the reason for their inception becomes invalid. These are the rules which should be changed or modified by mature people who understand that neither rules nor laws are sacred, but that they exist for the purpose of facilitating the lives and goals of the people who make them.

Learning Through Playing

A child usually is exposed to the concept of rules for the first time when she is given a game for Christmas or her birthday. An older brother or sister or a parent may sit down with her and "play the game" by reading the rules and trying to explain them to her. If she's between four and six, they may as well be explaining Sanskrit. If they become impatient at her lack of comprehension, she will be hurt and the game will be over, possibly never to be played again.

Most of the games marketed for children have inane rules which were probably concocted by a childless person or one who never plays with children. Whether or not the rules are sensible, a child under the age of five could just as well dispense with them and simply move the game pieces about to his own amusement.

Parents who fail to understand the workings of a child's mind may become concerned at his apparent disregard for rules and ruin all the fun. Thus, if a five-year-old boy's father decides to teach his son how to play a game of checkers, the following scene is likely to ensue:

Father: "Now, Barry, the checkers go on the black squares."

Barry: "I put *my* checkers on the red squares."

Father: "No, they go on the *black* squares."

Barry: "I want to put them on the red squares."

Father: "Look, I'm not going to waste my time with you if you won't play by the rules! Go outside and play and don't bother me anymore!"

93

The results of this episode of "play" are tears, hurt feelings, anger, misunderstanding, and possibly the beginning of a life-long rift between Barry and his father.

If Barry's father had understood how Barry's mind worked, and if his interest had been in having fun and establishing closeness with his son rather than in teaching him the adult rules of checkers, the scene could have gone like this:

Father: "The checkers go on the black squares."

Barry: "*My* checkers go on the red squares."

Father: "Oh. you want to play that my checkers go on the black squares and yours go on the red squares."

Barry: "Yes."

Father: "Okay, now, the way I play is that I move my checkers one black square at a time, and I can only move to a black square that is touching the black square my checker is on." (Illustrates moving his checkers.)

Barry: "*I* move this way." (Illustrates jumping his checkers in a haphazard way across the board.)

Father: "Okay, you move first."

The game could then have progressed with Barry changing his method of moving, not taking turns, and generally not observing any recognizable rules of the game of checkers. At length, when he decided the game was over, he and his father could happily put away the checkers, and Barry could have gone on about his other play. In this manner of playing, Barry and his father could have enjoyed fifteen minutes together, each treating the other with respect and consideration, and they could have grown closer together.

People who object to allowing a child to play without rules, instead of following the same rules adults follow, fear that such indulgences will cause the child to become egocentric, and that he will therefore never acquire knowledge of rules or regulations. Obviously, these objections miss the point. Young children play the way they do *because* they're egocentric. Trying to force them to be more mature doesn't lead to maturity, it only leads to hurt feelings, confusion, resentment, and possibly to delayed or arrested social development.

Adults who have strong competitive drives are often nonplussed at the cavalier attitude children between the ages of five and seven have toward winning. While children in this age bracket want to win, they have no concept that winning is an exclusive event. They are also unaware that winning is connected to finishing first, getting the most, or any other adult criteria of winning. At this age, playing and winning are about the same to a child, and all the children playing the game—however haphazardly they may go about it—believe they are winners, simply because they say they are. They also believe the game is over whenever they get bored with it.

If you point out to a group of kindergarten and first grade children that they can't all be winners when they are all merrily exclaiming, "I winned you!" you will spoil their fun and make them feel confused and diminished, but they won't understand your meaning. (And it really is a mean thing to do to them.)

Around the age of seven or eight, children begin to have some concept of rules and of competition. It is at this stage that you can help your child in several ways by spending some time with her playing table games.

Games become serious business at this age, and you can help your child immensely in her attainment of self-respect, self-confidence, a sense of humor, and the ability to think creatively if you join her in some simple games. You can set aside an hour or so a week to play a board game of some sort that you both enjoy, or you can be more flexible, playing whenever you and she wish to.

Whenever you play with your child, do so with good grace and good humor. If you resent the time you're spending with her, you either need some outside adult activities which are satisfying to you and which allow you to be relaxed when you're with your child, or you're displacing to your child some resentment you feel in other areas of your life. In either case, examine your feelings and try to resolve your own conflict rather than making your child feel guilty for your time and attention.

Choose games which are relatively simple, with very few rules and no complicated procedures. A simple board game with a fairly short route from start to finish, and only a few possibilities for detours or setbacks is best. Don't try to make the game-playing time an educational adventure by sneaking in arithmetic or reading tasks. This is supposed to be fun—for both of you. Anything either of you learns will be strictly because of what transpires between you, and not because of the composition of the game.

Explain the simple rules of the game to the child, such as "We move our pieces the number of places the spinner points to, and the first one to get to the winning spot wins." If you're throwing a die, help her count the dots, and when it's your turn, announce the number you've thrown so she won't feel left out.

As you move your token around the board, count aloud and move slowly, giving her an example of how it's done. When it's her turn, you may have to gently guide her hand along, counting as you go, until she gets the idea of moving steadily and smoothly from one square or hole or spot to another on the board. If you simply can't stand to play a game for the fun of it and have to feel you're making your child smarter, you can take pleasure in knowing that this bit of play helps in eye-hand coordination, counting skills, and gaining directional concepts.

As you play, forget all you ever knew about competition and winning. If she gets her token "home" first, be happy for her. If she has to go back a few spaces or all the way to her starting point, be cheerfully sympathetic. Remember the reason you're playing with her is to communicate some good feelings to her, not to teach her that winning is all important.

Don't become discouraged if she throws her newfound respect for rules to the winds halfway through the game and begins to move willy-nilly around the board toward the winning spot. Don't just sit there like a gloomy Gus, either. Start moving *your* token around just as she does. You may be surprised at what a deliciously liberated feeling you have when you do.

When you both reach the winning point on the board, congratulate her for winning, and put the game away for another day. Keep the time short, and your disposition calm and sunny, and you will probably find that you enjoyed it in spite of the immaturity of it.

In future games, you may either choose to play according to the rules, or to switch when she does and "do your own thing." But always begin by moving smoothly, counting, calling out the numbers, et cetera, so that she has a chance to play the traditional way. If she always stops the orderly movement during the game and reverts back to a more immature type of play, you may have chosen a game with too many restrictions, or she may not be ready yet for rules.

Try a simpler game which she enjoys and see if she can stick with it for a longer period of time. If not, no matter. Continue to play with her from time to time, and you will note that she will gradually follow your lead more and more as she grows older. Be sure you don't tell her how to play, although you can tell her, "I like to play *this* way," in a chatty kind of way. If she chooses to play her own way, don't worry about it. When she *can* play by adult rules, she *will*. In the meantime, enjoy her, and let her enjoy you.

Most children of this age like games which have spinners or cards which give them directions, such as "Go back two spaces" or "Spin again." They're not too fond of games in which one player sends another player back by landing his token on the same space at the other player's token. Children are suspicious of that maneuver until they're about nine, but they're willing to accept the authority of an impersonal card or spinner. They also enjoy the fact that the cards make them equals with adult players who may also draw a card telling them to go back three spaces.

If you play this kind of game, remember that your child will take his cue from you and react the same way you do. If you seem disgusted at your setbacks, he will be disgusted at his; if you groan in mock horror while obviously enjoying the game and its challenge, he will too. Most important, remember that the lessons your child learns about handling disappointment, frustration, triumph, and planning for goals while you and he are playing games will carry over into his entire life. How you and your child play a game will reflect how both of you live your lives.

If you regularly play table games with your child throughout his childhood, you will indirectly communicate more of your own values than you ever will through lectures or sermons. Traits such as generosity, fair play, firmness, flexibility, and good humor are all communicated through game playing. On the other hand, traits such as selfishness, pettiness, rigidity, jealousy, and shallowness are also communicated through games. The moral is to clean up your own act before you try to help your child acquire positive traits by playing games with him.

When a child has passed the age at which cheating is acceptable to you—which should be somewhere around nine—stop playing the game the moment the first indication of blatant cheating is noted. Allow a little leeway for lapses, but if you note a deliberate attempt on his part to deceive and give himself unfair advantage, promptly fold the game board, saying, "I can tell you're tired. Let's put this away till another time."

Don't mention his cheating. You'll embarrass him, and anyway he will be aware of the reason for the ending of the game. Let him save face and think you have associated his behavior with fatigue, boredom, or sleepiness. Be sure you don't sound or feel angry, and cheerfully go back to your own activities. Most children enjoy so much the one-to-one contact with a parent that they'll quickly eliminate cheating if it means their parent quits playing a game with them.

If he's ten or older, and persistently and knowingly cheats game after game, there is a problem that needs to be dealt with. First, make sure you've not been guilty of too much competition or emphasis on winning. Then set the game aside and talk to him. He may welcome an opportunity to get the matter into the open. Tell him that it distresses you for him to be so concerned with winning. Tell him it's much more fun for you to play to have a good time and not worry about winning. And if you, in your business or career, also believe that winning is essential to self-esteem, discuss your own aggressive drive with him and try to help him see that it's also important to just have fun in life, without the need for winning. You may discover some interesting and revealing information about him and yourself during the conversation.

If he seems compulsive in cheating and continues past your talks, it would be wise to seek professional help. The cheating isn't so important in itself, but the reasons for the cheating are. It's best to help your child lose irrational fears or anxieties which may cause him to need to cheat while he's young. Those same fears and anxieties will be much harder to lose once he's grown up.

Cheating In School

Now, lest you think you're home free just because you've helped your child learn not to cheat at games, think again. Remember school exams, and the notes written in ink on the palm of the hands, or on the ankle, so that when you pulled your sock down to scratch your ankle, you saw the answer to 7 X 6? Remember that?

And remember how you either sat very erectly in your seat so that your eyes had more range as you looked quickly side to side in a vain effort to see the answers on your neighbor's papers, or else how you sat hunched over your paper with your hands defensively curled around your answers to keep your neighbors from seeing them? Or perhaps you were more generous and pushed your correct answers toward the edge of your desk so your less prepared classmates could copy your work. It hasn't changed today. And neither have children.

There are still those who can't or won't do adequate work

99

and who try to benefit from the work that smarter or more efficient classmates do. In elementary school, junior high, senior high, college, and graduate school, the age-old situation still exists: there are the haves and there are the have-nots. There are those who study and do their homework and prepare for tests, and there are those who can't or won't and who ask others for help.

Many times, the haves are not the brightest children, but the most conscientious. And sometimes the brightest children are bored with the mundane nature of their schoolwork, and simply don't do it because they find it beneath their intellectual ability. Sadly, whether they fail to study or learn because they are too intellectually deficient to absorb the information or because they are so intellectually superior that they become easily bored, the final result is the same: they both fail to acquire the information.

It is for this reason, as well as for reasons of integrity, that children should be dissuaded from cheating in school. They may pass the exam by cheating, but they surely won't know the material. If your child is one who cheats on exams and in daily schoolwork because he is bored with the material and believes it to be unimportant, he may be cheating himself out of a successful future.

Many times parents encourage their children to remain in arrogant ignorance by ridiculing the intelligence of the teachers, and by implying or actually saying that their children's teachers are jealous and intimidated by the children's superior intellect. Thus, if a child fails to learn basic concepts in school, while displaying precocious intellectual curiosity at home, a short-sighted parent may sigh, "George is so much brighter than his teachers that he simply can't relate to them."

Or, "George's teacher is black, and George is so accustomed to white teachers that he can't do his best work any more."

Or, "Of course, since George is the only Jew in the class, he feels discriminated against. And it does seem peculiar that

George gets so many zeroes on his daily grades when he's obviously so bright."

These and similar comments will teach George one thing—that he is a special case, and that his performance in school is the responsibility of his *teacher*, and not his own. He will hear that he is simply a passive, superior sponge which may or may not absorb knowledge, depending on his teacher's ability to recognize and cater to his specialness.

These parents may intend to make their child feel good about himself, but what they actually do is cause him to be ill-prepared for a college or a career in which everyone else is as bright or brighter than he, and in which nobody is impressed by his intellect, his religion, or his color.

Many people avoid dealing with the mundane details of life because they associate doing so with being ordinary—like everyone else. In their determination to be superior, they may fail to acquire basic skills that would allow them to achieve true excellence in their careers. And many of these superior failures encourage their children to follow in their footsteps, never realizing the foolishness of their philosophies or the tragedy they are perpetuating.

If your child is truly intellectually gifted, try to place him in a school which will challenge his intellectual potential while at the same time demanding reasonable effort on his part. If a more stimulating school environment is impossible, don't allow him to use his superior intellect as an excuse for remaining ignorant.

Sympathize with him for the boring nature of his school-work, but demand that he do his own work and that he learn the basics which he so despises. Remind him that boring work is dull, but not awful, and that he, like everyone else in the world, will from time to time be subjected to situations which are less than stimulating. Impress upon him the fact that truly superior people force themselves to tolerate some necessary chores which are ordinary rather than exciting, and that people who refuse to do anything unless it is stimulating usually remain very ordinary.

Rather than cheating out of laziness or unwillingness to tackle work that is not challenging or stimulating, your child may cheat out of real or feared inadequacy. In either case, the problem needs to be dealt with promptly. Before you try to solve the problem with your child, however, ask yourself a direct question and answer it honestly. If you should discover that your child's intellect is only average, or perhaps below average, can you accept that and help him develop it to its full potential? If you are college educated and above average in intelligence, can you accept and encourage a child who may never go beyond high school?

On the other hand, if you were unable to finish high school, either because of economic reality or academic deficiency, and you have always hoped your child would realize the dreams of higher education you once had for yourself, can you accept the possibility that he may live his life pretty much as you have lived yours?

Given that your child has no learning disability, can you be happy with a child who is of average or below-average scholastic ability? Be sure you can honestly answer "Yes" to that question, because your acceptance of your child must be firmly rooted, no matter what his academic potential is, before you can deal with the problem of cheating because of real or feared inadequacy.

Getting Professional Help

Many times professional testing is required in order to distinguish between real and feared inadequacy. This is usually best administered by a psychologist rather than a school counselor, simply because school counselors don't have the time required for the extensive testing necessary to pinpoint a specific problem. Furthermore, a psychologist is trained to interpret the *pattern* of many combined test scores, rather than a few test scores themselves, and is more likely to spot scores that are low due to anxiety, depression, or neurological dysfunction than is a school counselor.

A psychologist trained in testing and working with children will also look at the pattern of individual responses. Does the child consistently have correct responses to test questions up to a certain level, and then fail all those administered subsequently? Or does he have spotty hits and misses, with easier items missed and more difficult ones passed? Does he know who Genghis Khan was, for instance, but not know how many eggs are in a dozen? Does he correctly copy geometrical designs while looking at them, but fail to remember what they look like when he turns the card over? Do his eyes begin to water while he's attempting to reconstruct a design with colored blocks, but not while he's drawing figures? Does he fail to correctly answer mathematical problems, but accurately remember a series of seven or eight digits? Can he repeat the numbers in the series backward but not forward?

All of these and many other questions are points that a psychologist will watch for in determining if a child is mentally dull or if he is plagued by anxiety, depression, visual difficulties, auditory difficulties, organic dysfunction, or some other problem.

Sometimes a child will show smooth and consistent learning up to a certain testing point, and then have spotty correct and incorrect responses beyond that point. A little sleuthing may uncover the fact that the testing point in question corresponds to a grade level during which the child's family made a traumatic move or during which the parents were divorced, there was a death in the family, the parents were experiencing significant marital discord, or some other anxiety-producing event occurred.

Like a distance runner who starts out smoothly and then steps on a sharp rock and bruises his foot, the child may continue to limp emotionally after the trauma and fail to function as smoothly or as efficiently as he once did. Since each grade level becomes more difficult, information that was not learned in the earlier grades becomes cumulatively disabling, and he may finally find himself unable to continue until he fills in the earlier lost material.

Growing up before your children do

In cases such as these, a combination of tutoring to fill in the academic gaps and psychotherapy to heal the emotional bruise may fairly rapidly get a failing child back on the track. Many times the psychotherapy has to precede the tutoring for awhile because the same anxiety and depression which prevented learning in school will prevent learning under a tutor.

A conference between psychotherapist, school counselor, parents, and teachers is helpful at this point, so that everybody concerned can coordinate their input in helping the child overcome his difficulties. Patience, understanding, and cooperation on the part of the entire adult team will usually help a child with this kind of difficulty regain his self-esteem and his ability to progress in school at his optimum rate.

In other cases, testing may show that a child has continued to learn information presented to him orally, but that he has begun to decline in learning information presented visually. This decline in learning usually takes place after the third grade, when children begin to do less seatwork with material at closer visual range, and begin to depend more on material printed on the chalkboard, which is further away from them. A child whose vision is less than perfect will therefore begin to learn less, but be unaware that other children can see better than he.

Many such children simply become perplexed and discouraged because their classmates are giving correct answers, and will conclude that they are inherently deficient. Usually they feel saddened and anxious when they make that conclusion, as well as fearful of their parents' displeasure when they discover what a stupid child they have. They may become more boisterous in a defense against their own sadness, or they may become withdrawn and subdued.

In some children, the problem isn't a matter of visual acuity, and standard eye charts may not indicate a problem at all. It may instead be a problem of visual perception or visual memory or visual association, which are different matters entirely. For example, a child may be able to see the letters or

104

numbers on the board, but he may have difficulty keeping them in his memory long enough to look back at his paper and copy them. Or the symbols on the board may appear to move up and down, making it very difficult to concentrate. Or he may not be able to see any integration between the letters or numbers, so that they are meaningless to him.

Again, these are problems that become cumulative with each grade level, and by the time they are acute enough to come to the attention of parents and teachers, the child may have so many emotional problems produced by his learning problems and his belief in his inadequacy that there has to be some psychotherapy along with the other professional help.

If you discover that your child has some sort of emotional or organic problem which needs professional attention, don't act as if he is a defective object to be worked on by other people. Treat the need for psychotherapy as you would treat the need for allergy treatments or physical therapy to correct imbalanced muscles. Be matter-of-fact, cheerful, and cooperative, without being anguished or guilt-ridden or inquisitive. His therapy, whether with a specialist in developmental vision, speech and hearing, or in psychotherapy, is between him and the professional and is not something he should discuss with you.

If you find yourself spending sleepless nights wallowing in guilt over real or imagined neglect which you fear may have caused or contributed to his problems, find your own psychotherapist and discuss your anxieties. But don't add to your child's burdens by dumping your own on him.

Are You Forcing Them To Cheat?

If you discover that your child has no learning problems and no organic problems to account for anxiety in school and possible cheating on school exams, then the focus comes back to good old Mom and Dad, the people who get all the blame and seldom any of the credit. Are you putting so much emphasis on grades that your child believes you won't accept an average or below-average grade? Are you only noticing him when he makes a superior grade? Are you punishing him when his grades are lower than you think he is capable of making?

If so, you're almost forcing your child to cheat in order to gain your approval. Be honest with yourself about what good grades really mean to you and to your child, and start focusing on the child rather than his grades. A child may do poorly on a test for reasons other than ignorance, for example, and parents must be realistic about that.

He can have a bad cold and feel so miserable that he doesn't do well. Or the test papers may have been so poorly mimeographed that he actually couldn't make out all the questions accurately. Or he may have sincerely studied the wrong material. Or anxiety may make him forget everything he knows until the test is over. There are many reasons why a student may do poorly on a test, and not all have to do with his failure to study or to learn.

Many parents who return to school to finish their own education discover their attitudes about children's test grades change dramatically when they are having some of the same experiences. Continuous failure, of course, is an indication of some problem, but occasional failure should be looked at for what it is. It's embarrassing, but it's not a catastrophe. It may mean that the person taking the test didn't study enough, but it doesn't mean the person is lazy or stupid. Even failure of an entire course doesn't mean failure in life.

I think it would be good for every child and every parent to remember the many famous and successful people who have failed in school. Winston Churchill and Albert Einstein, for example, both failed some school courses, and Charles Schulz, the creator of *Peanuts*, once failed every school subject for the entire year.

Some children who develop test anxiety have to be given permission to fail before they can begin to perform up to their ability. You may have to sympathetically tell them, "A lot of people learn well, but don't take tests well. It doesn't matter.

The important thing is that you *learn*, not that you make a good test grade. You know and I know and the teacher knows that you have learned the material. It doesn't matter what grade you make on the test, only that you have learned."

A child with disabling test anxiety can best be helped by taking her to an early movie the evening before an exam, or by involving her in some relaxing game or family outing. If she has some relaxing diversion shortly before an exam, she will be more relaxed and less apt to freeze up at the time of the test. In extreme cases, a professional trained in clinical hypnosis can help a child relax during school examinations and recall learned material.

When Accelerated School Classes Cause Cheating

There are two other situations in which children may be tempted to cheat in school. One is when they are placed in accelerated classes which move too rapidly for material to be absorbed, and the other is when a child has been able to "coast" for several years without having to expend much energy and then finds himself in academic situations in which he suddenly has to put forth effort.

Accelerated classes are both a blessing and a curse. They are more fun, more interesting, and more challenging to bright, inquisitive children. But they can become ego-boosters to teachers who compete with other teachers to cover more ground in a shorter amount of time to prove their superiority as teachers. They can also become part of an academic caste system in which students in accelerated classes are labeled "bright" and students in regular classes are labeled "dumb."

If an accelerated class is taught by a teacher who stresses creative thinking and who supplements the regular material with interesting and innovative projects, the children will naturally move quickly and will find joy in their learning because they will be stimulated and challenged.

However, if the teacher of an accelerated class simply tries to rapidly force-feed new material to the class, without regard to their absorption or stimulation, there is likely to be a feeling of joyless desperation on the part of the students to do whatever is necessary to keep up. In this kind of situation, there is a temptation to cheat in order to remain in the accelerated class, especially if the teachers imply that only the "smart" students are in the accelerated classes, and if being an accelerated student is a status symbol for the child or for his parents.

Some children can adjust well to a very fast pace. Some can adjust well to a fast pace in some subjects, but not in others. And some very bright children need more time in all subjects to assimilate learned concepts before they move on to new ones. If being in a regular classroom carries the stigma of failure, however, or of being "dumb," a child may frantically try to stay in an accelerated class, and may feel humiliation and despair if he is moved to a regular class from an accelerated class.

If you have a child in an accelerated class who cries or becomes tense with anxiety over impending tests, ask yourself how important it is to you to be able to say, "My child is in an advanced math class." Do you feel smarter when you let other people know you have a smart child? And would your child be any less smart if he were in a regular classroom where he learned the same material six weeks later? Does he need an opportunity to master one concept before he moves on to another? Is he in a situation in which he may be tempted to cheat in order to keep up with the rest of the class?

Certainly, if your child is in an accelerated class and happy, contented, and doing well, he should remain in it, but don't confuse "accelerated" with "smarter" and create problems you don't need. If it appears that a rapidly moving class is doing your child more harm than good, it would be wise to explain your thinking to him and suggest that he go to a regular classroom.

Cheating After "Turning Dumb"

The other situation, that of a child suddenly arriving at a point at which schoolwork becomes a chore, is a little sad. It may happen—and most usually does—when a child who has found elementary school a breeze enters the relatively more demanding world of junior high school. Or it may not happen until sometime during his college career. When it does happen it is devastating in its impact, and the child experiencing it usually believes he has reached his intellectual peak and is now on the downhill side. Children in this predicament feel frightened, ashamed, and desperate, convinced they they have suddenly become dumb, and unaware that they simply have reached a point at which they can no longer learn without working.

Unless they are helped to understand that even geniuses have to study and work at learning new, difficult material, they may resort to cheating in a mistaken belief that it's the only way they can continue to make their former good grades. They need reassurance that while they once could do well without studying, the fact that they now have to study doesn't mean they have suddenly become stupid.

If the child who has abruptly "turned dumb" is a boy between the ages of fourteen and seventeen, look at his pants and see how much leg is showing between the hem of his jeans and the top of his shoes. Many boys have such extreme and sudden growth spurts during these years that their energy all goes into growing. Their brains literally don't have the necessary energy to learn, and they will temporarily "turn off" until their bodies get back to a normal growth pattern.

A child entering a drastic growth spurt changes almost overnight from a learning, thinking, reflective adolescent into a shuffling, slack-jawed zombie whose glazed eyes seem to be empty of thought or intellect. Be patient. Feed him, love him, see that he gets lots of sleep, and don't expect very much of him for a while. Resist nagging him, and one day a few weeks later he will wake up bright-eyed and several inches taller, ready to resume living and learning.

During that time he will probably be dimly aware that he is doing poorly, and be ashamed of his grades and confused about what is happening to him. Again, be patient. Tell him quite simply that his body is undergoing a lot of changes, all tremendously important, and reassure him that he's just as bright as he ever was. Promise him that in time he will be through the process of sudden spurts of growing and that he will not lose his mental abilities in the meantime.

Don't let a child of this age become hysterical about grades or their future impact on college acceptance. Encourage him to do his best without cheating, and promise him that it will get better with time. Remind him that college admissions offices are aware of the impact of adolescence on learning. If his grades in the last two or three years of high school are reflective of his scholastic ability, most colleges will focus on those years and not on the years when his grades are more apt to be erratic due to "acute puberty."

As in all other matters, the key to guiding your child around all the obstacles and pitfalls which might induce or encourage him to cheat in order to succeed is for you to have a level of emotional maturity that allows you to function as an adult, while allowing your youngster to be the child. That's easier said than done, of course, just as everything else is.

To be mature enough to help your child grow up free of the need to lie, steal, or cheat, you have to like yourself and be proud of yourself and your accomplishments, while at the same time realizing that you are far from perfect. If you always strive to improve, while feeling pleased and satisfied with your progress, you'll find it easier to view your child's progress with a healthy perspective. You won't feel disappointed and frustrated when your child makes only a small step toward maturity. Instead, you'll rejoice that he is progressing normally, and you'll have faith in his eventual maturity.

If you are fully grown up, free of the need to have everything instantly the way you wish it to be, capable of working and loving and enjoying life, you'll be able to allow your children to be immature. You won't engage in endless bickering or fruitless power struggles or jealous pouting or ego-inflating demands. Instead, you will be relaxed and comfortable, able to enjoy your children without losing yourself in sacrifice for them, and able to guide and instruct them for their future benefit rather than your own.

If you are caught in a helpless whirlwind of emotions regarding childish lying, stealing, or cheating, and are unable to get some adult perspective on it so you know when to intervene and when to keep quiet, get some professional help for yourself. You'll *all* benefit!

Likely as not, the child you can
do the least with will do the
most to make you proud.
*   -Mignon McLaughlin*

Chapter Seven

JUST RELAX AND LOVE THEM,
AND YOU'LL ALL GROW UP OKAY!

If I had a hundred dollars for every time a parent has asked me, "How can I motivate my child to do what he is capable of doing?" I'd be the richest woman in the United States and Canada. If I had the answer to the question, I'd be the richest woman in the world.

The fact is that you can't motivate anybody to do anything. You can facilitate. You can allow. You can provide all the basic ingredients a person needs in order to achieve his utmost potential. But you cannot motivate a person any more than you can motivate the growth of a flower.

Being a parent and raising children is much like being a gardener and raising flowers. The main difference is that your crop is much smaller, thank goodness, but the principles are the same. And while an experienced parent, like an experienced gardener, might find the task easier, even a rank amateur can have beautiful results. It only takes loving attention, a lot of patience, and a small amount of know-how.

Suppose you were a novice gardener and somebody gave you a packet of assorted seeds. If you had good gardening instincts, you would carefully prepare a flower bed, loosening the soil and adding rich humus and other nutrients to it before you planted the seeds.

After the seeds were planted, you would keep the bed slightly moist so the seeds would germinate, and when the first tiny tips of plants began to push through the earth, you would put some sort of protective screening over them to keep animals from disturbing them. As they grew, you would continue to protect them from the elements, and you would provide judicious amounts of water and sunlight to aid their growth. You would keep them from the harsh burning rays of the sun, from flooding, and from the force of strong wind, but you would allow them to gradually become accustomed to the world as they became strong enough to tolerate it. If you noted some collapse of their young stems or yellowing of their immature leaves, you would provide some extra support or nutrition to help their growth. You wouldn't angrily jerk them out of the ground and throw them away because they weren't developing perfectly.

Unless you were an experienced horticulturist, you wouldn't know exactly what variety of flowers you were growing, but you would have faith that they would all develop as they were supposed to, and you wouldn't worry that they might blossom in the wrong colors or the wrong shapes. You also wouldn't have any need to hurry their development along. You wouldn't pull on their fragile stems or try to unfurl their curled leaves. You would simply watch them develop and enjoy their progress, noting that some grew faster than others.

You would also note that some were different shades of green than others, that some had hairy stems and serrated leaves, while others had smooth stems and leaves. Some might be short and compact, their dense covering of leaves attractive despite the lack of flowers, while others might be almost all angular stem and bud, with no particular grace or beauty. You would accept all their characteristics with equal pleasure, enjoying each for what it was, confident that each would be ultimately a thing of beauty.

When your flowers began to blossom, you would be delighted in discovering what you had been cultivating. You would admire the bright and sturdy little marigolds, the cheerful pansies, the shy violets poking their faces through their leaves, and the petite, multicolored dianthus. You would note that some of the gangly, ungraceful stems blossomed with the most brilliant and beautiful flowers, adding spirit and character to your garden. Each different flower would have its own unique beauty, with none being more important than its neighbor.

Being a novice parent requires about the same kind of mature tolerance for normal growth and individual differences. It's too bad that some parents aren't willing to wait and allow their children to blossom into whatever they are destined to be, without pushing or prodding or trying to force them into being different, or without trying to force them into blooming before they're ready.

A child, like a flower seed, contains within himself all the potential for ultimate growth and intellectual ability. If he is well rooted in family soil, nourished by love, acceptance, humor, firmness, good nutrition, and intellectual stimulation, he will naturally grow and bloom, fulfilling whatever his unique potential is.

Some parents can't leave well enough alone, however, and have to keep jerking on a child to try to make him grow faster or realize his potential sooner, instead of allowing him to develop at his own pace. Like a flower whose gardener keeps fiddling with its stem, trying to hurry it along, a child will quickly wilt and lose some vigor with such interference.

When that happens, his parents usually become alarmed and instead of realizing that their own impatience has caused the wavering growth, will redouble their efforts to "motivate" their child toward faster development. Children whose parents interfere with normal growth may finally bloom, but with less beauty and character, and some may never bloom at all, but remain stunted and unfulfilled.

Parents are more inclined to push their first child–since their egos are more attached to him–than they are to push subsequent children. They may encourage their child to walk early by holding his hands and walking with him before he's ready to let go and navigate by himself. They may rush him to give up the breast or bottle before he's had all the suckling satisfaction he needs. They may do all sorts of unkind things to him to get him to stop sucking his thumb–even though they themselves may still suck cigarettes.

They may push for bowel and bladder control before their child is ready, and berate him when he can't cooperate. They may expect mature behavior in social situations long before their child is able to understand what is expected of him.

By pushing a child to give up one stage of development before he is ready, and to prematurely move on to another, parents not only cheat their child of feelings of competence and mastery, but they cheat themselves of enjoyment of each developmental stage. By always wishing for what comes next instead of enjoying what *is*, they never experience the satisfaction of the moment.

They also create an anxiety in their child which may never completely leave him. Because his earliest experiences pushed him precipitately to levels of behavior he didn't gradually attain, he may always feel anxiety about his competency in any situation.

School Will Wait Until They're Ready

One of the most damaging things parents can do is to push a child to start school before he is ready. Probably more than half of all children are pushed to begin school before they are neurologically or psychologically ready, because their parents are overly anxious for them to get started. A child pushed to begin school when he isn't ready will be slow to learn to read—not because of low intelligence but because of immature central nervous system development—and thereby may begin a lifelong pattern of failure.

The ability to read doesn't simply come about by having letters and words presented to a child in a manner designed to teach him to remember them. And neither is reading something done solely with the eyes. Instead, reading is a brain function, and the brain, being part of the central nervous system, will not perform the reading function until it has

115

reached a certain stage of development. That stage may occur as early as the age of four years, but is more likely to occur sometime *after* the age of six years. In fact, there are authorities who contend that age eight is the earliest safe time for children—even gifted children—to start to school.

For some obscure reason, our school system has adopted a slightly hysterical belief that we can only hope to keep up with the Russians or the Chinese or some other power if we accelerate our educational process. Ever since the Soviet Union launched Sputnik I, we have ignored what we know about maturation and learning, and have frantically tried to cram too much too soon into young children. Instead of allowing them time to absorb and learn, we push them into new competitive situations before they are ready. Instead of allowing them time for exercise and relaxation during the day when they could get mentally prepared for more learning, we give them a quick twenty or thirty minutes in which to eat lunch–sometimes with a teacher standing at the front of the school cafeteria urging them to "Hurry! Hurry!" and blowing a piercing whistle if somebody talks out loud to a neighbor–and a short token "recess" during which organized games are played as a form of Physical Education. We are then surprised when we reap the results in high school graduates who can't read and college students who can't compose a coherent, grammatical sentence.

To try to teach reading to a child whose central nervous system has not yet reached the necessary level of development is as futile and as stupid as trying to teach calculus to a third-grader. When children whose neurological development is not yet at a reading-readiness stage are placed in school and expected to learn to read, they experience not only confusion and unhappiness, but they learn they are not as capable as their neurologically-ready classmates. Their academic futures are then almost dismally predictable.

By the time a child who prematurely entered first grade is neurologically ready to read, his classmates will have progressed to more complicated books, and he will still be behind. Parents and teachers who pushed him to start school too soon may be distressed at his slowness and may begin to push him even harder, and to talk about his "laziness," his failure to "try," and his "lack of motivation." They thus begin to criticize and condemn his normal rate of development as if he could or should be different then he is, and as if he could or should push some magical maturity button and speed up his own developmental process.

Since he won't have experienced the thrill of achievement not tainted by knowing his parents and teachers are disappointed that he didn't do it sooner, he will find no joy or pleasure in learning. And he will be acutely conscious that his parents and teachers consider him lacking in some way. If his school divides the better readers from the slower readers, he will be very aware that being a "Redbird" is not as important as being a "Bluebird" and he will be ashamed of his slowness.

As time goes on, he will probably continue to move slowly and without any excitement or enthusiasm for learning, since he will associate learning with feelings of embarrassment, inferiority, and frustration. Even when his neurological development has reached a level equal to that of his classmates, he will have long since stopped feeling equal to them in intelligence, and will have "turned off" to school. His early school experience may have been so frustrating, in fact, and his resentment toward his parents and teachers so intense that he may consciously rebel and refuse to give them the satisfaction of being pleased with his performance.

While his teachers and parents desperately wonder how to "motivate" him, he may simply concentrate on enduring his school years until he can escape. It may be years, and it may be never, before he feels intellectually equal to his peers and is willing and/or able to function at his full potential.

How much better it would be for this child and others like him if he could simply postpone entering the first grade until he was neurologically ready for reading at age seven or eight. How much better it would be for him to enter school fully equipped for the learning experience to be gained there, with enthusiasm and self-confidence.

Why in the world do we allow local school boards to determine the age at which every child is ready for school? And why do people feel embarrassed at having a child who is ready to read at seven or eight instead of at six? What difference does it make? Is there a prize for the parent whose child starts school at the earliest age? Are today's parents so lacking in things to compete over that they must push their children to begin school before they're ready?

To be sure, there are children who are physiologically, neurologically, psychologically, and sociologically ready for reading as early as five years of age. It stands to reason, in fact, that if the age of six is the *average* age at which a child is ready to begin school, there will be children below that age as well as children above that age who will reach the level of maturity necessary to begin reading. It is far more unusual for a child to be harmed by too-late entry into school, however, than by too-early entry.

Typically, the child who's not quite ready to begin school at the time the local school board or state legislature says he should is a boy whose birthday falls between January and September. The closer to September his birthday is, the less likely he is to be neurologically ready for school before his seventh birthday. A lot of girls are not ready for school at the age of six, either, but for some reason boys seem to have a little slower neurological development than girls, so they are more apt to start school too soon.

Any child not neurologically or cognitively ready to read would benefit greatly from spending another year in kindergarten, where he can gain more social maturity and experience more adventures to aid him in understanding concepts and ideas when he begins reading. The best "reading readiness" program, in fact, is one which introduces children to new experiences, not one which endeavors to teach meaningless symbols. A child who encounters the word *tractor*, in print for example, will have a much better comprehension of the word if he has actually visited a farm and experienced a

tractor. He will similarly comprehend and more quickly recognize printed words such as *tiger, giraffe, canoe, airport,
museum,* and *factory* if he has actually seen those things and
experienced them in his life.

Absolutely vital to learning to read for most children is a
good grounding in phonics—the sounds of letters. You can
help your child at home, whether or not his kindertgarten
class has phonic instruction, by playing games with letters of
the alphabet. You may have magnetic letters which you can
attach to the kitchen refrigerator, or you may have some
textured letters which your child can play with, feeling them
as he manipulates them.

He can thus learn with you while you peel potatoes that
the S is a snakey letter making a "Ssssss" sound, that the P is
a motorboat letter making a "Ppppp" sound, and that the T
tiptoes on its "Ttttoes."

If he has lots of rich experiences, visiting different places
and seeing different things, if you read to him often so that he
knows that reading is fun, if he is allowed to develop at his
own neurological pace, and if he learns phonics in a relaxed,
gradual way, he will begin to read when he is neurologically
ready as surely as the sun will come up tomorrow, with no
effort on anybody's part.

When he first puts together the sounds of two or three
letters and pronounces them as a word, he will be excited and
entranced with his new skill. He may first read a billboard
sign saying, *Car Wash* or he may read the words on a
building's door saying, *In* or he may read *Dad* or *Mom*
someplace.

At that point, and not before that point, he is ready for
"real reading." If he arrives at the stage of neurological
readiness while he's still in kindergarten, he'll be that much
ahead when he begins first grade, and his head start will go
with him throughout his school career. He will continue to
enjoy learning, to enjoy reading, and to enjoy his own
achievement.

Frequently when parents are advised to keep their six-year-old in kindergarten for another year because he is obviously not ready for reading, they will exclaim with dismay, "But he'll be so far behind!"

Behind what? Behind whom? What is the race? The object of education is to learn, not to be in a particular grade level at a particular age. Paradoxically, the child who starts later may finish earlier than he would if he had started earlier. This is due to the fact that children who begin school before they are neurologically ready may have to repeat more than one grade because they become so discouraged they stop making an effort.

The child who was fully ready for the first grade when he started, on the other hand, may move ahead in the later grades because of his superior performance. He may either graduate earlier from high school or be eligible for a three-year college program because of advanced courses in high school.

Even if there is no advancement in school because of starting first grade after the age of seven, what difference does it make? Is it so vital that a child be pushed to begin a formal academic program which may cause him unhappiness and frustration, and which will almost certainly cause him to have less self-esteem and less academic success than he would otherwise have? What's the purpose of the rush? Is it because the parents want their child to grow up and leave as soon as possible, and can't stand the thought of having him with them an extra year?

The real reason, of course, is that parents use their children's developmental progress as a measuring stick of their own superiority as parents. Surely, they reason, a child who is ready to read at the age of five or six must have parents who are uncommonly intelligent and outstanding, while a child who doesn't read until the age of seven or eight must have dull and inferior parents.

For some reason, the same parents who reason in that manner also feel triumphantly proud if their children cut teeth early or walk early or become toilet trained early, as if precocity in their offspring's physical development was a reflection of superior intelligence in the parents.

How silly and tragic that belief is. In actual fact, a child may show precocious physical development and be of average intelligence. Another child may talk, walk, and read at a later age and be of superior intelligence. And in either case, the child's intelligence belongs to him, and not to his parents. Geniuses may beget average children, and average parents may beget geniuses. Remember that Albert Einstein was four years old before he talked, and even at the age of nine, he was still not able to speak fluently.

It's often very difficult for parents to decide whether or not their child is ready for first grade. Many times, teachers will encourage early school entrance in the belief that children need the "motivation of competition." That makes as much sense as it would to remove a cast from a broken leg before it had completely healed on the theory that it would heal faster if it were in competition with the unbroken leg, but a lot of children have entered school prematurely with that rationale behind them.

A child's pediatrician may judge a child's readiness for school according to his health and physical size, and leave the decision up to the parents. Grandparents, aunts and uncles, neighbors, older children in the family, and perfect strangers will all have different opinions, each with a reasoning which may sound sensible. The final decision, however, must rest with the parents, who usually have fairly good intuitive feelings about the matter.

For example, does your child still seem to require an afternoon nap? Does he still suck his thumb when he's tired? Does he need to sit and cuddle with you in the morning before he can start his day? Does he seem unusually sensitive to pain? Does he sometimes wake with startled, jerky movements? Is he small for his age? Can he accurately copy a diamond-shaped geometric figure? Does he seem more shy than the average child?

These are just a few of the indicators of possible central

121

nervous system immaturity, and any one could be a cue. There are others, usually so subtle they can't actually be pointed to with certainty. If there is doubt, let his birthdate be your guide. If he will not be six years old until after January before school starts in September, be cautious. If he will not be six until sometime in the summer before school starts in September, be *very* cautious. It is better to err in the direction of being overly cautious and having him stay another year in kindergarten than it is to err in the direction of pushing him to begin first grade before he's ready. The worst that can happen if he stays a year more than necessary in kindergarten is that he will become a class leader and come to see himself as such. Since the world needs more leaders, I don't see anything wrong with that.

Prior to the time that state legislators decided that all six-year-old children were ready to read, our educational system recognized the developmental stages of childhood and allowed for entry into first grade in the middle of the year instead of in September. Thus, a child whose birthday was in late Spring or early Summer could enter first grade in January along with other children whose birthdays fell around the same time, and all started with about the same neurological development.

Now, a child with an October birthday may begin school the following September along with children with August birthdays, giving October's child almost a full year's headstart. It's senseless to expect the August child to have the same readiness, but that's how our educational system works. This is one instance in which you don't have to join 'em if you can't beat 'em, however, so don't let anybody make you push your child to begin first grade before he's good and ready. Remember that he's good enough already, but he may be far from ready.

Don't Use Them To Compensate For Your Disappointments

Even parents who don't push their children to begin

school before they're ready may push them to achieve out-standing excellence in sports or music or some other field, thereby robbing the children of feelings of accomplishment. These are the parents who ask, "How can I motivate my child to do well in his music lessons?" or, "How can I motivate my child to play football when he's so obviouly suited to it?" or, "What will motivate my child to take pride in his appearance?"

What these questions really ask, of course, is, "How can I get my child to make me proud?" or, "How can I get my child to reward me for all the sacrifices I've made?"

All parents, even the best, feel a reasonable right to expect something for the time and money and effort they invest in bringing up their children. But some parents expect their children to compensate for every disappointment they've ever had in life, so that they can turn to the world and say, "See, I may not be the best looking person in the world, or the smartest, or the wittiest or most interesting, but as all can see, I am a good parent. The proof of what a good parent I am is the fact that my son, the first baseman of the Westchester Little League, the good-looking kid who never picks on any other kid but who flattens all bullies who pick on him, the kid who can play flawless Chopin, the kid who is unfailingly polite to old ladies and who is never seen picking his nose in church, is the same kid who always makes good grades in school and who always finishes every project he starts. That's what a good parent I am, and that is the legacy I leave the world."

Parents make all sorts of bargains with their children in an attempt to push them into being points of personal pride. They bribe them to make good grades with money for each A on their report cards; they stand over them in relentless determination while their children agonizingly and miserably practice musical scales; they "help" them with their homework and the next day eagerly ask, "How did we do?" They are hurt and offended and frightened and humiliated when their children fail at anything. These parents are par-ticularly mortified when their children appear to be disinterested or resistant to attempts at structuring their level of success.

Are You Teaching Them To Be Losers?

The paradox is that the parent who wishes the most fervently for his child to succeed in the world and who tries the hardest to "motivate" his child in that direction is usually the parent who very unwittingly creates a child with very little motivation or self-confidence. In fact, it is very easy to create a guideline for parents titled, "HOW TO TURN YOUR CHILD INTO A LOSER."

First, always lecture him sternly about the importance of doing everything well. Make the credo, "Anything worth doing at all is worth doing well" one that he hears many times, whether in relation to his school work or making his bed or feeding the dog or pulling weeds or buttering his bread. Criticize him liberally after each task and point out to him each and every mistake he makes, lest he overlook any. Always be scrupulously honest and never tell him he has done well when he hasn't. Always use the same criterion to judge his work that you would use to judge your own or another adult's work.

Second, punish him consistently for failures, so that he never forgets them. If he makes a failing grade in school, punish him severely. If he fails to do well in a sporting event, berate him publicly so that he will experience the humiliation of being disgraced in front of friends and spectators. Demand perfection and absolute success from him and refuse to be satisfied with anything less.

Third, never listen to any excuses, however logical they may appear. Be sure he knows that your loyalty is first to the school, his coaches, his teachers, and the neighbors, and lastly to him. Make public all his failures so that he will experience the full brunt of his mistakes. Tell his grandparents and the neighbors and the members of your bridge club when he fails, so that you will receive their sympathy and he will receive

124

their condemnation.

And lastly, when he is an adult and seems to have little loyalty to you and seems to have little recollection of the sacrifices you made for him in spite of his failure to succeed in school or in sports, turn to all your friends and bitterly proclaim how well you understand the full meaning of Shakespeare's "How sharper than a serpent's tooth it is to have a thankless child!"

Maybe you don't want to create such a total failure. Perhaps you would rather create a moderate failure. In that case, your rules would be somewhat different.

For a moderate failure, it's not necessary to demand absolute perfection. Instead, tell your child, "I don't care what your grades are, so long as you do your very best."

If you say, "So long as you do your very best" with the proper intonation, you can convey the silent message you really mean, which is, "I know and you know that your very best is better than anybody else's, and unless you do better than anybody else, it will simply break my heart. So if you want to break your mother's heart, go ahead and play around and bring home a C on your report card. It's alright, I'll hide my pain."

You can also, if your child fails to come in first at a swim meet or at any other competitive event, say with sacharine sweetness, "Don't feel bad, darling, I know you did the best you could."

She may not have felt bad at all until you suggested she should, but she will remember the next time and be appropriately tense and rigid so that she will forever after continue to come in second.

When she takes part in a dance recital or a music recital, be sure to tell her teacher how much you appreciate her patience with your child, and be sure you say it within your child's hearing, so that she doesn't forget that you and her teacher both know how negligent she is in studying and practicing. Make it obvious to her that she is tolerated, but not admired.

125

Be *very* understanding of her problems. Have frequent conferences with her teachers and her counselors and her coaches and her team leaders. Make sure they understand that she is a trifle lazy and a trifle uncaring, but that *you* care and make every effort to help the poor thing "realize her potential," and that you are desperate for ideas which may help you "motivate" her.

As much as possible, and as often as you can, imply to her and to others that your health, your marriage, and your sanity are seriously impaired because of your child. Try to steer a course between sainthood and heroism in your martyrdom, but humbly accept any accolades you may receive for your unstinting sacrifices.

Above all, be sure that you know what is best for your child, in spite of what her teachers, school counselors, physicians, or other professionals may tell you. What do they know, anyway? Who are they to tell you that your child is normal, when it is perfectly obvious that she is lazy and indifferent? And how can they tell you to turn your attention to your marriage or your friends or a hobby when your child so desperately needs all the help she can get?

Let Their Lives Belong To Them, Not You

The point of all this unseemly sarcasm is that you can best help your child to achieve her full potential by providing the best possible atmosphere in order for her to grow. Give her lots of love and firm boundaries, give her wholesome, nutritious food eaten in a calm, happy atmosphere, offer your encouragement when she needs it and your help when she is obviously having trouble, and then butt out.

Let her make her own mistakes, and suffer her own failures. Let her decide for herself what she wants her goals to be, and then let her decide how hard she wants to work in order to attain them. Let her achievements and accomplishments truly belong to her, attained because she wanted them, and not because she wanted to please you.

If she is a child who has few goals, few things which she wants to work for, accept that. She may be a good audience, a good appreciator of what other people do. And when something comes along which interests her and which she believes in, she may go after it with a zeal that will amaze you. Remember that Peggy Guggenheim is famous not for the paintings she painted, but for the paintings she collected. She was not an artist, but an appreciator of art, and she gained a fortune and a respected reputation because of her ability to appreciate the talent of others.

In the garden of your family, your child may be a gentle and delicate gardenia which offers pleasure to others simply by existing. Or she may be a defiant zinnia which dares the sun and throws itself at the world with headstrong abandon. Or she may be a slow-creeping, fragrant jasmine, winding her way slowly but steadily along her own path, not very showy or outstanding, but tenacious and dependable.

Whatever she is, love her and appreciate her for what she is—a unique individual deserving of respect and acceptance. To best do that, of course, you must first see yourself in that light and respect and accept yourself as an individual, not just as a parent. You are deserving of appreciation and love just because you exist, and not because of the superiority of the children you produce.

If you find that you always introduce yourself to others as "Johnny's mother," if you find your conversation centering around your child and his school, baseball team, or other activities, if you have no triumphs other than those achieved vicariously through your child, you're probably creating problems for yourself and for him. He is likely to respond to your over-involvement by showing tension and anxiety. He may cry over minor frustrations. He may become ill before exams at school. He may be hateful and rude to playmates. He may refuse to compete with other children and withdraw to solitary activities, or become aggressively competitive and make enemies by his belligerent attitude. He may become excessively dependent on you, unable to make a decision without your help, or he may rebel against you totally, and reject anything you offer him.

Do you really want that? Do you really want to go off to college with your child and "motivate" him? I didn't think so. What you most likely want is a sense of importance and of worth. At least, I hope that's what you want, because feeling important is necessary for all of us, from infancy to the grave. Sometimes we act as if that need is unnatural, and we say things such as, "She's just trying to get attention" in a scornful way, as if wanting attention is something shameful or sick.

The fact is that wanting and needing recognition is basic to healthy functioning, and the person who denies that need in himself will be maladjusted and frustrated, and will create unhappiness for other people. The wife who is "Mrs. John Doe" instead of "Mary Doe" quite likely depends on John to do something worthy of recognition so she can enjoy some of the spotlight. If John fails to achieve or advance in life, Mary may feel bitterly resentful because she has been cheated of her sense of importance. Or, if John succeeds but his success is solely his own and Mary isn't allowed to share it, she may then turn to Johnny to give her the sense of success she needs as a person. If Johnny is an outstanding achiever, she will be a "good mother." If he is only average or below-average, she will have "failed" as a mother.

To be sure, there's nothing wrong with feeling important and recognized as a good parent. Parenting is the most important job in the world, and the future of mankind depends on how well today's parents perform their job. Being a good parent is indeed something worthy of respect and pride.

But the danger in relying on being a "good mother" or a "good father" for one's *total* self-esteem is that the child's achievements become the measure of the parent's worth.

A good parent is one who is calm and relaxed in the midst of all the hubbub of an active family. A good parent is unfailingly mindful of a child's sensitivity and never says cutting, sarcastic things to hurt a child's feelings. A good parent provides the best possible nutrition and health care for all members of a family. A good parent maintains a balance between parental sacrifice and individual needs, and finds time for hobbies and interests that are not child or family related. A good parent maintains adult relationships that are satisfying and enriching, has fulfilling intellectual stimulation, and personal goals that are never completely set aside. A good parent is liberal in his praise of his child and extremely stingy with criticism. A good parent tells his child that he is loved many times a day with words, smiles, and hugs. A good parent sets reasonable limits for a child and refuses to allow him to go beyond those limits. A good parent demands to be treated with courtesy, and treats his child with the same courtesy he demands for himself. A good parent loves his child just as he is, and has faith that he will follow the examples set for him at home.

Now, if you're all those things, you're a good parent, and I'd like to get your name and address and see about canonizing you immediately. Even if you come close to being all those things, you deserve all the importance you feel. You should feel proud of yourself even if your child made a D in spelling last semester. Even if he has a voice like an angel and refuses to sing in the church choir. Even if he sometimes forgets to turn in homework.

On the other hand, you're not being a good parent—even if your child has straight A's and is captain of the football team—if you're living through him, and if he's achieving those things for you rather than for himself. I know you *say*, and I know you sincerely *believe* that you only want what is best for *him*, but it would be better for him if you taped books for the blind, or raised money for cancer research, or volunteered at your local library, or learned karate, or studied Arabic, or got a part-time job, or *anything* that got you pulled back a healthy distance from his world.

Remember that your child's life is precious not just because of its physical viability, but because of its emotional viability. Your child, like you, not only has the right to enjoy his own life, and his own achievements, he also has the responsibility for doing so. Your greatest achievement in life may be in allowing him to own himself, and in setting an example of how that's done.

Before I got married I had six theories
about bringing up children;
now I have six children and no theories.
-John Wilmot, Earl of Rochester
(1647-1680)

Chapter Eight

IF YOU'RE HAPPY, THEY WILL BE, TOO!

What kind of family do you have? I don't mean how many parents or how many children or how many relatives you have, but what kind of team is your family? Do you remember the old Esther Williams movies in which swimmers moved through intricate patterns filmed from above and resembled the changing patterns of a kaleidoscope? Or the June Taylor Dancers on the old Jackie Gleason show who did the same thing on stage? Or, for that matter, how about the circus trapeze artists whose careers and/or lives depend on the split-second cooperation of the other high wire performers?

Does your family have that kind of well-timed cooperation? Or is it more like a Keystone Cops comedy in which everybody is running around bumping into one another and not accomplishing anything? Or, worse yet, is it like a zoo in which incompatible animals have been housed together, all snarling and spitting at one another in suspicious fear?

Once in family therapy, I saw a family in which the parents and five children were continually screaming and attacking one another. They snarled sarcastic, hurtful accusations whenever possible at each other, they screamed vulgar, obscene invectives that would have shocked the most hardened pornographic dealer, and they had absolutely no sense of loyalty or love toward one another.

The parents sought counseling because of the scholastic failure of their children and because they couldn't stand to live in the same house with the children as they grew into adolescence and became totally uncontrollable. It quickly became apparent that the parents in this family had been so isolated from the children by their own marital conflict that the children had grown up almost like feral children, with virtually no guidance from their parents.

The parents were uncomfortable with the shouting and screaming and fighting in their home, but they attempted to handle it by screaming louder than the children, becoming furious at the lack of response, whipping whoever was easiest to catch, and then retreating into their bedroom where they screamed at each other.

The children, needless to say, were unhappy, anxious youngsters, who felt no love or support from their parents. In failing to put boundaries on their children's behavior, the parents had created discord, anxiety, and hostility. The hostile habits were so ingrained, however, that it was impossible for any of them to immediately change their behavior, and in fact, none of them had any incentive to do so.

Extreme situations require extreme measures, so I used a little "paradoxical intention" therapy with them. I told them that a lifelong habit of cursing and shouting was very difficult to completely break, and that in fact they might never lose their need to be obscene, rude, and inconsiderate. I asked them, however, to save all their hateful remarks for an hour immediately after dinner, and at all other times to phrase their remarks to one another in polite, friendly tones.

They were then to gather in one room for an hour each evening and deliberately be rude and hateful to one another. They were to use every vulgar expression they knew toward one another, and they were to avoid any polite or supportive remarks. The father was appointed as the monitor of these hour-long sessions, and he was to stop any child who forgot the rules and started being polite. He was to insist that all his children during this hour speak to one another and to him in a belligerent, hostile manner, and he was to particularly insist that they speak in obscenities.

The children obeyed reluctantly, since they were forced
to be aware of their own foul tongues during the session. The
parents hated the hour and tried to find a way to convince me
of its futility, but their pride in being cooperative with their
therapist was on the line, so they too obeyed. Within about
three weeks, the ridiculousness of the entire situation reached
an intolerable peak, and the father self-righteously exploded,
"I don't care *what* Betty Stewart says, you will *not* use
language like that ever again in this house!"

In that moment, he took the control he had abdicated for
so many years, he asserted his authority which was long
overdue, and he communicated his involvement with his children, which was all they had been trying to get.

I have seen other families who not only didn't scream at
one another, they didn't speak to one another much at all.
Instead, they seemed to float around their houses like silent
wraiths, each caught up in his or her own thoughts and
feelings, and solitary within their own worlds.

These are the families who may not eat together, may not
spend time together, may not be involved with one another at
all. We usually think of these kinds of families as either very
wealthy, with beautiful-people parents who are continually
jetting around the world while their children are served by
hired domestics, or as very poor, with parents who have to
leave their children to their own devices while they scrabble
for a meager living.

The fact is that uninvolved families may be of any social
or economic class. They also may not be physically separated,
but appear to be a close-knit, caring, "together" family. They
may attend church together, go on vacations together, have
their meals together, and watch TV together. But their physical togetherness may belie their emotional separateness.

Getting It All Together

Everybody in the world, including children, has two lives.
We have the external life which is apparent to everybody else,

and we have an internal life which is known only to us and to those who are very close to us. A child's external life involves his playmates, his school, his family, and his activities. His internal life involves his dreams, his hopes, his fears, and his reactions to everything in his external life.

To the extent that a child or an adult has nobody with whom to share his internal life, he will feel isolated and lonely. Whether or not a person feels lonely doesn't depend on the number of people around him, but on the amount of shared feeling there is with other people. It's for this reason that some people who live alone feel far less lonely than other people who may live with several others. The alone person may have one or two people in her life with whom she can share feelings, either in person, by phone, or by letter, while the person living within a large family may have nobody who knows his feelings or thoughts.

Children, having no choice about where they live or with whom, have to simply make do with what they have. They will either be surrounded by people who guide them in learning to share their feelings, or they will be surrounded by people who never learned that skill themselves. Lonely, isolated parents teach loneliness and isolation to their children, whether or not they are surrounded by numerous people.

The ability to express feelings is probably the single most important communication skill that binds people together and gives them a sense of existence and of importance. Some people never acquire adequate skills in communicating feelings. Others either learn to communicate feelings in the normal process of growing up with their families, or they learn it in the process of psychotherapy. Learning it within the family is easier, less costly, and gives a person more time in his life to use it.

Learning To Express Feelings

A lot of adults sincerely believe they are able to communicate feelings, when in fact they don't even have feeling words in their vocabulary. Ask a person with no feeling-communication skills how he *feels*, and he will say, "I feel that she is right about that," or, "I feel that there is a need for some more discussion about that," or, "I feel that ...." something or other.

Those are not expressions of *feelings*, they are expressions of beliefs or opinions. A feeling is or can be expressed in one word, and the word "that" is never included in the communication of a feeling.

When people in psychotherapy are working toward learning to communicate feelings, they will advance from the "I feel that..." stage to the stage in which they say, "I feel upset."

The word "upset" is probably used more often by more people with less explicit meaning than any other word in the English language. It can mean "angry," or "afraid," or "disgusted," or "frustrated," or "repulsed," or "anxious," or any one of a hundred other feeling words. Using the word "upset" to communicate a feeling is about as useful as using a charcoal stick rather than a sharp-pointed pencil to record checks you've written in your ledger. It indicates that some activity is going on, but precisely what it is will be blurred.

After an adult in psychotherapy becomes aware that the word "upset" isn't adequate, he then becomes aware that he honestly doesn't know *what* he feels, because his feelings have so long been buried under a layer of what he thinks he should feel, or what he believes other people feel, or what he fears he may feel if he really looks.

So the first process in learning to communicate feelings is to identify the feeling, and that's probably the most difficult thing adults who are not familiar with their own feelings have to do. To distinguish between embarrassment and humiliation, to distinguish between anger and fear, or to distinguish between pain and resentment takes much introspection and willingness to probe and explore one's own psyche. It also requires a degree of sophistication in knowing the exact meaning of all those feeling words. Sometimes people in psychotherapy who are college graduates or who have law or medical degrees find themselves turning to dictionaries to ascertain the exact meaning of a feeling word so they can be absolutely sure they are accurately communicating their exact feelings.

There's another necessary process in the development of emotional communication skills after the mastery of identification and labeling, and this step is vitally important. It is the necessity to have another person *accept* what you are communicating. Only then does a person experience the feeling of existence and of importance. Otherwise a person who expresses his feelings, however precisely, will be like a tree falling in the forest with nobody around to acknowledge the fall.

How many times has this happened to you: You have had a very important experience which you need to tell somebody about. You call a friend or a relative and relate the experience and say, "I feel terrible about it," or, "I'm so worried about it," or, "I'm awfully scared," and hear from them, "Well, that's a silly way to feel." Or, "You shouldn't feel that way, that's stupid." Or, "Why in the world do you feel that way?"

Do those responses make you feel any more sure of yourself? Do they make you feel important? Do they make you feel that your feelings matter? Probably not.

You would probably feel much calmer or more satisfied with yourself and your friend if you heard something like, "Gosh, that must have been awful," or, "I can understand how you would feel like that," or, "I'm awfully sorry you feel so miserable."

In fact, if you heard your own feelings accepted and acknowledged, you might very quickly discover that you didn't feel that way any more, and you might begin to perk up and say, "I guess it really wasn't so bad," or, "Now that I've told about it, I don't feel so scared any more."

You wouldn't have changed your feelings because your friend tried to force you to, but because he accepted them as valid in the first place, and accepted your right to have them.

Children have even fewer vocabulary skills than adults have to express and communicate their feelings. They also have even less confirmation of their own importance in the world and of their existence as people who matter. But their feelings are just as real and just as important, and they have just as much need as adults to have them accepted and acknowledged.

Very small children will communicate feelings with symbolical words or behavior. A child who feels hurt and angry and left out, for example, may wet the bed in the unconscious hope that somebody will interpret his feeling message and accept it and him as valid and of worth.

A child who has absorbed a lot of tension in his home and who instinctively knows that his parents are very insecure may refuse to leave home and go to school. He may become ill, look pale, or become terrified. Again, he will unconsciously be communicating his concern and feeling of strained protectiveness toward somebody whom he feels needs him.

The adults in his world usually become angry at him when he refuses to go to school, and that will cause him to become even more anxious and determined to stay home and protect his adult. We call that "separation anxiety" and usually label the anxiety the child's. But if the child could verbalize his feelings, he would probably say something like, "Look, it's not *me* who's afraid to be a separate person, it's my parent. I can't leave home and become separate until and unless my parent who needs to be needed so much becomes a separate person."

Many of the feelings children would like to express are very normal and very healthy, but parents and professionals tend to discount the feelings and try to change them rather than accept them. Sometimes they are discounted by being *described* or *diagnosed* rather than being accepted.

Psychologists and psychiatrists, for example, have a way of discounting normal and healthy feelings as if they were uncommon phenomena. When a child hates his brother or sister, for example, we refer to it as "sibling rivalry" because nobody likes to call it "brotherly hate." Parents become unhappy and full of despair when they see one of their children filled with resentment and hatred for a brother or sister. And when all the children in a family seem to bear grudges against one another, the unhappiness of the parents is pathetic, as they plead with their unhappy children, "You must *love* one another!"

Parents usually compound any resentment their children feel toward one another by trying to force them to feel love instead. The first time a toddler bashes his baby sister's head with a toy, his mother is likely to run to him in anguish and exclaim, "Oh, no, you mustn't hit Baby Sister, you must *love* Baby Sister! Give Baby Sister a kiss!" The poor toddler then will dutifully kiss his baby sister while plotting mayhem in his little heart, and the stage is set for—organ music, please— SIBLING RIVALRY.

If the toddler's mother said instead, "You feel angry at Baby Sister. You don't like Mommy to love Baby Sister, but I can't let you hit Baby Sister," at least he would know that somebody understood how he felt. And if the mother correctly interpreted his attack on the baby as a need for more attention from her, she could try to provide for his increased needs without neglecting the baby.

To understand how a child feels when a new baby arrives, imagine that you live in a society in which men frequently have more than one wife, but that you and your husband have a good relationship and you expect to be his only wife. Then imagine that your husband suddenly brought a new wife to your home without consulting you, and that the new wife was helpless, incompetent, and totally useless. Imagine your surprise and outrage if your husband showed the new wife a lot of attention and complimented her inordinately when she did the least little thing, and ignored the far superior things you did.

You would probably be rather rude to the new wife, and less than helpful. Imagine how hurt you would be if your husband was displeased with you and said, "You must *love* my new wife. You should *help* her. She's here to stay, you know."

And if you said, "But she's worthless, and you give her a lot more attention than you give me, and I'm a good wife," and your husband said, "Don't talk like that about her. You must *love* her," you would probably sizzle with resentment and jealousy and never feel any warmth toward her.

If your husband said, however, "I know it's not the same now that she's here. And I'm sorry that I've been spending so much time with her and not enough with you. I promise I'll try to spend more time with you, and you know how much I value you and our relationship. But it's important to me to have two wives like all the other men have, and we have to adjust to the change and live happily together," you might not feel much better about her coming, but you would feel a little less resentful and jealous. You might in time come to like the new wife and actually be willing to help her adjust to your home.

The same is true of children who resent and are jealous of brothers and sisters. If you acknowledge and accept a child's feelings and tell her something like, "I know your brother is a pain sometimes, especially when he gets into your things," rather than punishing her for disliking her brother, she may very well begin to feel a little more tolerant toward him.

One of the more interesting changes that occurs during play-psychotherapy with children, in fact, is that a child may enter the play-therapy room full of hostility and resentment toward a sibling. She may act out her hostility and jealousy by playing with the doll house and the dolls in it, having the brother in the doll family fall off the roof and be knocked unconscious and then drug off to the desert of the sandbox by ferocious doll dogs. In the sandbox desert, the brother may be run over by toy Army tanks, get shot by doll Indians, mauled by hairy apes, and flung through the air from a cannon. His body may then be buried in the sand with a flourish, and left there while the child turns to an inflated clown and punches it in the nose several times.

When all the animosity has been expressed, verbalized by

explicit announcements such as, "I hate my brother! I wish he would blow away!" and accepted with equanimity by the therapist, the brother doll is usually tenderly rescued from his sandy grave, brushed off, kissed, and reinstalled in the doll house where he is happily welcomed by his doll sister.

At the end of the play-therapy session, when she receives her stick of gum—with which she is bribed to leave—she will usually ask happily, "Can I take some gum to my brother?"

Eventually, with enough opportunities to vent her resentment and jealousy toward her brother, with her feelings accepted and acknowledged without judgement or censure, her feelings toward her brother will become evenly serene, with occasional anger and competitive jealousy, but without continuous, painful, and self-defeating hatred.

Very little children, who are consumed by feelings they can't describe, will frequently use colors to try to communicate how they feel. Almost universally, children associate the color red with pain, and a sensitive child with a limited vocabulary may weep, "I feel all red inside!"

Slightly older children may be able to draw a picture of their feelings, and a parent doesn't need a degree in psychology to interpret them. I remember one child, for example, who was the "apple of her mother's eye" and who was smothered by too much attention, too much involvement with her mother, and too much attention paid to her clothing, her hair, and her relationship with her friends. This child painted a picture of a pretty flower growing in a flowerpot, with a happy sun smiling down on it all. Then, with telling accuracy, she painted black prison bars in front of the flower, the sun, and the entire happy picture.

Obviously, nobody deliberately causes their children to grow up emotionally restricted or distressed by painful feelings which they cannot communicate to others. Neither does anybody wake up one morning and think to themselves, "I believe I will see how lonely or isolated I can make my child." But many parents inadvertantly do just that because of their own upbringing and their own inability to teach their children skills which they don't have themselves. If you would like your children to grow up experiencing the feeling of belonging, of being important to the world, and of relating to other people in a satisfying way, make sure that you are able to do so yourself. Then it will be very natural to teach those skills to your child.

You Can Do Harm In Spite Of Good Intentions

All this business about the importance of the family in determining the future emotional health of the child is probably making you feel very defensive and possibly vaguely guilty. I don't mean to cause those feelings, and in fact I think most caring parents do a remarkable job of helping their children grow up well-adjusted and with self-respect and self-confidence, especially since most parents have to create their own models as they go along.

While there are, to be sure, a few parents who are just plain mean and sadistically sick and who should never have had children in the first place, most parents who cause problems for their children do so in the mistaken belief that they are being good parents. They are apt to be too self-sacrificing, too absorbed in their children's lives, too ready and willing to help, too quick to offer solutions, too generous with gifts and money, and too readily available.

Let me give you an example of the kind of well-meaning, misguided parent who is likely to cause problems for her children. She is a composite of all the mothers and fathers I have ever known who create the traits they are most trying to prevent in their children. Let's call her Joyce.

There is no doubt that Joyce is a good mother. She is such a good mother, in fact, that she makes other mothers slightly uncomfortable. She is always slightly disheveled and obviously spends no time on herself. She and her husband haven't had a romantic vacation or a weekend or an evening alone together since the first baby was born.

Joyce doesn't work, of course, although she has a good

education and worked prior to her children's arrival. She also doesn't have much time for reading or for hobbies, since she is so involved with her children. She no longer has any interest in any of the things she used to enjoy doing by herself.

Joyce is extremely active in the PTA and in the church, where she teaches a Sunday School class. She alternates each year so that she is always teaching one of her children's classes. She is also a Cub Scout Den Mother, a Bluebird leader, and Home Room Mother for both her children's elementary school classes. She carpools, of course, and is always willing to drive if another mother is unavailable.

When her daughter had to have cookies to bring to the Valentine's Day party in the second grade, Joyce was up until past midnight baking tin after tin of cookies and then decorating them with red and white icing, in spite of the fact that she was so ill with viral pneumonia that she frequently had to lie down on the cool kitchen floor–which, of course, was spotlessly clean–to rest her feverish body. (Several mothers voiced their anger at her for sending germ-laden cookies to school, but Joyce nobly dismissed their anger as jealousy.)

When a driver is needed for a school field trip, Joyce is always ready to volunteer. When library helpers are needed at school, Joyce can always find one day a week to donate. When volunteers were needed to screen prospective first-graders for visual-perception problems, Joyce was one of the first mothers to put her name on the list.

Joyce visits the school often and holds lengthy conversations with her children's teachers about their work. She is on a first name basis with the Principal, and frequently offers suggestions for the betterment of the school. She is always aware of the projects her children's classes are working on, the homework assignments they have, and their daily progress in school. She always helps both her children with their homework assignments right after dinner each night, and she questions them after school about their daily experiences. She often surprises them by showing up at the school cafeteria and joining them for lunch. If either of her children is in a school play or school program, she can be depended upon to show up and assist the director, offering suggestions and direction.

Joyce's children could pose in a children's clothing ad with their perfectly coordinated shirts, skirts, and slacks. Her children's shoes and socks are spotlessly clean, their shoestrings are always new and crisp, and even their wash-and-wear clothes show ironed creases on the sleeves.

Their rooms are equally worthy of a magazine ad in their color-coordinated perfection and neatness. Their toys and games all look just-bought, and there are never signs of messy play in their rooms.

Does Joyce sound like anybody you know? If you recognize the mother of one of your children's friends, feel sorry for the children, and pat yourself on the back for escaping the Perfect Parent Pox. But if you recognize yourself, sit up and pay attention.

If you have no interest in life beyond your children, you will smother them. If you are married and fail to take the time and energy to keep your romance alive by getting away from your children at least one evening a week and one weekend a month, you're doing your children a disservice, as well as your marriage.

If you have no hobbies, no jobs, no goals outside your children through which you can find satisfying achievement and accomplishment, you will rob your children of their own achievements and prevent them from growing as individuals. If you are overly involved in your children's world, you will rob them of their own place in it, and they will resent your intrusion and possibly rebel by failure.

Just as the two extremes of great wealth and great poverty are likely to produce the same self-centered personality traits in children, so do the extreme opposites of parental negligence and parental absorption produce the same passivity or self-defeating rebellion in children.

There is a four-point continuum, in fact, along which parents may place themselves. They may be negligent, with children who never accomplish much because they never experienced encouragement or regard from their parents. They may be average, with children who have average achievements, or above-average devoted parents, with children who have above-average accomplishments. Or they may be obsessively devoted parents who rob their children of independence, either pushing them to be neurotic, deviant, or, less likely, to be geniuses.

The fact that you're reading this book removes you from the negligent category, since negligent parents wouldn't spend the time trying to learn how to be better. So you're probably average, above-average, or obsessively devoted in your involvement with your children.

Since there's nothing wrong with average or above-average achievements, if the person achieving them is satisfied and happy, the only thing you have to be concerned about is whether or not you fall into the obsessively devoted category. And the best way to avoid that is to be sure that you have a life that belongs exclusively to you and nobody else, as well as a life that belongs to you and some other significant adult in your life.

You're Important, Too!

If you have those two separate lives, the life you share with your child won't be so all-encompassing, and it will stay in its proper perspective. To be sure, your role as parent may often have to take precedence over your other roles. Your romantic second honeymoon will have to be postponed if your child needs emergency surgery. Your weekend away from home may have to be forgone if that's the weekend your child plays in the Little League Championship game. Your coat will have to last another winter if you and your child both need one and she's growing and you're not. Your dream of ballet classes may have to wait until your child's teeth are straightened.

But you can have some of your own dreams, some of your own needs met, while still being a good parent. You can spend a morning playing tennis and pick up cupcakes at the bakery to deliver to the school birthday party without damaging your child's personality. You can attend classes all day and come home and throw together a skillet dinner that will be tasty, nutritious, and quick, without losing your standing as a caring mother. And you can dress up and be glamorous and go out for an evening and leave your children with a competent sitter without having to call home three times to make sure Susy isn't crying for you. You can, in short, create a family atmosphere in which everybody's needs and feelings are recognized and given importance.

By being involved with your children in a healthy way, giving their needs and feelings respect and acceptance, you can help them grow in independence and self-confidence. By setting boundaries beyond which you will not allow your children to trespass on your needs, you will enable them to feel relaxed and secure in your willingness and ability to stay in control. And by paying attention to your own needs and goals of achievement, you will release your children from your relentless attention and allow them to live their own lives and feel pride in their own accomplishments.

Now, I must warn you of something. If you stop competing with other parents for the Parent of the Year Award, you will create a lot of jealousy among other parents, and they will express their jealousy as criticism. If you stop running along behind your school-aged children with a broom and mop and start cheerfully telling them to clean up their own dirty tracks, somebody will look askance at you. If you start spending a lot of your day at a woodworking hobby or researching political candidates or taking art lessons, the "Cookie-Baking Mamas" on the block will surely find you subversive.

Furthermore, you must be prepared for a lot of kids hanging out at your house instead of going home. If you are friendly, accepting, and relaxed, pleased with your own accomplishments and your ability to juggle several roles at once, you will attract children like a magnet. They will much prefer coming to your children's home, where there may be some clutter and disarray, with fruit for snacks instead of decorated gingerbread men, than going to their own homes and tempting the displeasure of a mother who has spent the entire day cleaning and polishing and baking and who will resent any intrusion into her clean, perfect world.

Nobody Is Loving *All* The Time!

And while we're on the subject of the Perfect Parent Pox, stop feeling that you have to love your child all the time! What makes you think you can or should always love your child? Only a real dyed-in-the-wool masochist really *enjoys* changing dirty diapers, losing sleep, going without new clothes in order to pay the orthodontist's bill, having a restricted social life because the family comes first, and giving up all the million and one other things that good parents give up for their children. And every normal parent occasionally thinks with some longing of being a single person with time and money to spare instead of being a parent with neither enough time or money to do the things they want to do.

One of the best mothers I've ever known was a woman with six children between the ages of three and thirteen. She once told me of the tremendous load that was lifted from her when she made the discovery that she didn't have to always love her children. Barbara said she and her husband Joe rarely found time for themselves, and that she had begun to feel less and less enjoyment in her children. She had kept her guilty secret to herself, however, believing that she was an abnormal mother and that her husband would lose respect for her and be horrified at her wickedness if he should ever know her true feelings.

One morning at breakfast, however, her patience wore through with her thirteen-year-old son, and she fled from the kitchen in rage and confronted her husband in the bedroom.

"I hate Bobby!" she cried, "I just *hate* him! He's ugly and obnoxious and smelly, and I wish I'd never had him!"

She threw herself on the bed and sobbed disconsolately,

sure that her marriage was over, that her husband would leave her and take the children with him—and she hoped he would. Instead, he lay beside her and held her close, and when her sobbing had subsided, he said matter-of-factly, "I hated Bobby last week, but this week I hate Karen."

"What?" exclaimed Barbara.

"I said," he repeated evenly, "this week I hate Karen. Last week I hated Bobby."

"Why do you hate Karen?" asked Barbara in confused wonder.

"She's got the smartest mouth of any kid in town," said Joe, "and there are times when I would smack her in the mouth, but her teeth have cost us too much to knock out."

"How can you hate your own child?" asked Barbara weakly.

"Easy," said Joe. "I can hate 'em 'cause I love 'em. I love them more than I hate them, so I don't feel bad when I hate them. I thought everybody hated their kids now and then."

Barbara was silent for a moment, and then laughed softly, "Last month I hated Casey. He was a real pain for a while."

"Yeah," smiled Joe, "I hated Casey last month too. But he shaped up and now he's fun to be with again."

After a few similar honest talks, in which she and Joe shared anger and laughter over their feelings, Barbara relaxed in the knowledge that it was normal and natural for a loving parent to have moments of hateful feelings toward his or her children. She also found that she was much more patient with her children and more tolerant of their childish inadequacies once she was able to honestly and guiltlessly think of how much they sometimes irritated her.

It was especially calming to be able to voice her feelings to Joe, who always accepted them with calm good humor for what they were: honest feelings of anger and disgust toward children she loved. Together, she and Joe shared both their pride and their distaste for individual children, never feeling negative for very long toward any particular child, but always able to honestly and often with humor say how hateful they felt when the feelings were there.

To be sure, if you have persistent hateful feelings toward one particular child, or toward all your children, something is wrong, and you need help. But short-lived feelings of resentment, anger, and disgust are normal and healthy emotions and should be accepted as such. Parents are first and foremost human beings, not Olympian gods, and they must accept their own human emotions as normal. Only then will they be able to accept their children as less-than-perfect beings and allow them the same human feelings.

The ability to express negative feelings about—not toward—a child is particularly important for parents with learning disabled, hyperactive children. I'm not going to go into hyperactivity or its companion, learning disability, in this book, because the topic requires far more coverage than I can give it here. If you have a learning-disabled, hyperactive child, you already know it. And you don't need a treatise on the causes or treatment, because you undoubtedly have heard it many, many times before.

What you may need, however, is permission to occasionally become angry at your child for being so concrete that he can't generalize one set of circumstances to another. You may need permission to feel frustration and impatience when he can't understand why you've imposed a rule upon him, and when your explanations are never comprehended. You may need permission to feel jealousy when your friends' children learn effortlessly and mature smoothly. You may need permission to feel hurt when all your effort and time and love isn't noted, much less appreciated.

Remember that the opposite of love isn't hate or anger; it's indifference. If you didn't love your hyperactive child, you wouldn't become so frustrated and angry at him. If you weren't very concerned about his future, you wouldn't sometimes wish you hadn't had him. Don't be ashamed of your feelings of anger and resentment, they're only natural and healthy. Don't express them to him, however. It will only make him feel bad and make you feel guilty.

Get away as often as you can where you can breathe without listening to see what he's doing. Even if you have to sell your grandmother's heirloom silver one piece at a time to afford competent babysitters while you get away for a weekend, it's worth it. Your sanity is more important than the investment.

If you can find one in your area, join a parents' club and exchange hair-raising tales of the exasperation of being the parent of a hyperactive child. While you should explore every diet, every allergy possibility, every possibility of vitamin or mineral deficiency, and every psychotherapeutic aid available to you, allow yourself the luxury of becoming angry and disgusted from time to time.

It's better to go into your bedroom and pound your mattress in frustration when you are particularly distressed with your child than to remain with him in tight-lipped fury. He will sense your displeasure, even if you don't voice it, and be confused and uneasy. It's better to get it out of your system so that you can accept him and help him with the love you actually have for him.

Parents also need to help their children accept and deal with the normal hostile feelings they sometimes have toward their parents. It's just as normal for children to feel hateful and resentful toward their parents as it is for parents to feel hateful toward their children. If we teach children to feel guilty for being angry at their parents, we will compound the feelings by driving them inward, and they will be expressed as depression, rebellion, or anxiety.

Expressing Anger Constructively

To every family I see in therapy, I recommend getting a family punching bag–one of those large canvas bags filled with sand that hangs from the ceiling. If the bag is large enough and firm enough, it will last for years and through several children. The smallest child in the family can bang on the bottom end of the bag when he's angry with his older brothers and sisters or parents, and the other members of the family can hit whatever area is at their height.

You can draw faces on the bag and kick them. You can hit it with your fists—while wearing boxing gloves—or you can take a stick to it. You can drain away your anger at your boss or your teacher or your mother-in-law or your nosey neighbor or the man at the garage who probably cheated you or the President or anybody else you may feel anger toward. It helps if you talk while you hit the bag, saying what you would like to say to the person you're angry at. They won't hear you. They won't be hurt. And you'll feel a lot better.

Usually, when I recommend the punching bag to people, their first response is, "But it won't change anything!"

They're absolutely right. Hitting a bag won't change the world situation or a school grade or get you a job promotion or cause businesses to be more fair to you. But hitting a bag will keep you from going around tense and grim and depressed, and possibly will keep you from getting headaches, ulcers, or more serious side effects of unexpressed anger.

People tend to be more afraid of anger than any other human emotion. People approach anger as if it were a living thing, a snarling monster which can harm them, instead of just another feeling. The fact is that anger can either be a healthy, constructive emotion that inspires people to find cures for diseases or to end proverty and despair, or it can be a negative emotion that leads to murder and destruction.

Most people fear what they would do if they didn't "control"-meaning suppress-their anger. Buried beneath the calmest exteriors are usually fears that anger let free would cause a destructive rampage. People who have never done more than raise their voices in anger often have secret fears that they might "lose control" and do serious destructive harm. They fail to distinguish between "controlling" which is to choose the direction anger will take, and "being controlled" which is to fear the emotion in any form.

I once saw in therapy a gentle woman who never expressed any negative feelings, and feared her own possible destructive potential. Since she was suffering from serious gastrointestinal problems brought about by repressed anger, however, she was willing to take any advice. After some time spent with her in which she accepted the *idea* of anger, my "prescription" was that she rent a room in a cheap Galveston beach motel, let her frustrations and hostilities have full sway, and then pay the motel manager for any damage she had done to the room.

With determination borne of desperation, she followed the advice, and when she came back for her next appointment, she had a pink-cheeked contentment I'd not seen in her before.

"I really went ape," she confessed. "I yelled and screamed and ran around the room and threw things and hit things and generally had a terrific time."

"Did it cost you very much?" I asked.

"Well, not really," she laughed. "When my rampage was over, I'd thrown the bedspread on the floor and the pillows were all over, and I'd overturned some chairs, but I guess real destructiveness just isn't in me."

Real destructiveness isn't in most of us. We might break some glass, or overturn some things, or dent some things, but most of us would stop short of real mayhem. Interestingly enough, the people who can't fantasize destruction, who can't pretend they're talking to superiors and "telling them off" are more likely to actually lose control and do the things they can't imagine.

So begin early to teach your children to substitute an inanimate object for people when they're angry. It's better to hit a punching bag than a person. It's better to kick a plastic wastebasket than your brother. It's better to throw clods of dirt at a tree than to say rude things to your mother. It's better to draw an unbecoming picture of your sister than it is to hit her. It's better to write your dad an angry letter and then tear it up than it is to shout at him.

When a child can control the direction his anger takes, he

is truly in "control" of his anger. But when children or adults refuse to express anger at all, then the anger is in control of them. Truly "controlled" anger is anger expressed in a planned and deliberate manner, not anger that builds up and finally explodes in a wall-smashing blow with the fist, or in a death-tempting race down the highway.

Like all other expressions of emotions, once you let a feeling out, you may find that you don't feel that way anymore, or that your feeling is still there, but it's not so intense and painful. Sometimes, draining off all the intense rage can allow a person to find a possible solution to the anger and it may then be possible to sit down with the person you've been angry at and talk rationally and calmly.

In a family in which anger is accepted and controlled through acceptable direction, a child will feel free to become angry at his parents for some punishment or decree he thinks is unfair, glare balefully at them, march silently to the garage and punch the bag for several minutes, and then return calmly with no comment from anybody.

His parents may have smiled at one another when he began hitting the bag, but they will feel relaxed and accepting of his anger and the way he is choosing to express it. When he returns, the child may talk to his parents and try to negotiate a better deal for himself, but he will be free of his earlier hot anger. And in a healthy family, his parents will listen and give his feelings and thoughts respect. They may decide they've been unfair, and change their decree. Or they may decide to stick to their guns, but explain their reasons again without anger.

They will *not* allow their child to speak to them with rudeness or belligerence, nor will they speak to him that way. And if they feel that he's being particularly factious, or if they feel particularly disgusted with him, they will tell each other, and perhaps hit the punching bag a few times themselves, but they will not be rude to him or deliberately hurt his feelings.

When Anger Is Destructive

I can almost hear some parent protesting as he reads about how wonderful it is to allow a child to express anger, "My child expresses nothing *but* anger! He bullies everybody and hits his sister and seems to hate everybody!"

Constant anger, continuous hostile aggression, and relentless physical tension is a different matter than constructive expression of occasional anger. In a very young child, hostile aggression is a way of communicating anxiety or depression. Perhaps you're not spending enough quality time with him, reading to him, playing with him, or being close to him. Perhaps there is some family "secret" that makes him sad, but nobody talks about it. He may "know," for example, that a loved grandparent is dying, even though everybody has been careful to keep it from him.

In some cases, a child may be excessively hostile because he has been chosen by the family to act out their hidden angers. When this happens, psychotherapists say that the child is the family "scapegoat," and if the child is taught appropriate behavior in therapy, the family may very well turn their attention to another child in the same family and make her the new family scapegoat.

Almost always, if there is more than one child in the family and all but one are happy, well-behaved children, while one is a constant troublemaker, the chances are that the parents are unconsciously causing that child's behavior by their own repressed emotions. The child needs help, to be sure, but the parents need help more than the child does so they can learn to deal with their own antisocial impulses without having to have them acted out by one of their children.

It isn't necessary for a family scapegoat to be one of several children. An only child can also be used by one or both parents as a scapegoat. You can sometimes spot parents who scapegoat their child by the way they tell one and all how bad their child is, how much a trial she is, and how they are unable to make her "behave."

153

Frequently, scapegoating parents blame each other for the child's behavior, with one saying the other is too permissive, or too strict, or too inconsistent, or too negligent, or too overprotective. Thus the child becomes a pawn which the parents move about in an effort to conquer each other, while each is secretly delighted at the other's discomfort at the child's behavior. These parents, may, by the way, be divorced for several years and remarried, and still continue to scapegoat their child.

When scapegoating parents tell of their child's misdeeds, there is always a curious note of pride in their voices because having the *worst* child on the block becomes rewarding for them. Scapegoating parents are frequently passively aggressive people who unconsciously force others to act out their own destructive or aggressive impulses for them.

When these parents talk about their children, they do so with an air of helplessness, as if the child were much stronger and smarter than they. They seem to ask, "Can I help it if I have produced a child who is so quick and so inventive that I cannot control his behavior?"

An example of such an attitude and such a result was Maurice, a man who requested therapy because of sexual impotency. In the course of therapy, Maurice presented himself as a man who was always "done in" by the rest of the world. His wife was cruel to him, his parents had neglected him, his business associates cheated him, his customers were ungrateful to him for the many extra things he did for them, and the world at large stood ready to take advantage of him, while he was always quick to help a friend or a stranger in need, never asking anything for himself, always allowing himself to be used and abused, always sure that he was the most honest and long-suffering person in the world.

He discussed his two-year-old son on his first therapy session, referring to him as "*He*," in a tone of special awe. It quickly became apparent that "He" had a terrible temper, was selfish, unreasonable, uncontrollable, much smarter than the average child, and destined to be either president or a criminal when he grew up. When he spoke of "Him," Maurice's face was creased in a concerned and angry frown, but his voice was full of pride and envy.

"He," of course, was simply acting out all his father's repressed anger and hostility toward the world, while his father remained passively aggressive and vicariously enjoyed the misbehavior of his son. As Maurice learned to directly express his considerable hostility toward others and to stand up for himself rather than allowing himself to be pushed around, "He" miraculously became a much more cooperative and even-tempered child.

If extemely nonaggressive, conforming parents have a child who is very hostile and aggressive, there is a strong chance that they are unconsciously provoking their child to act out their own aggressive impulses and are getting vicarious satisfaction from watching him be "bad."

There are other cases in which parents use their children as objects to hurl at the world because of the parents' hostility. If they are bitter about injustices they believe they have suffered, they may train their children to be hostile and antisocial in order to hurt other people. Such was the case with ten-year-old Marilyn, the only child of a middle-aged couple who constantly bickered and fought. The father was a millionaire many times over, and his whining wife had quite admittedly married him in order to gain financial security. He was a very rude, belligerent man who believed that no woman could love him because he was fat and bald. That his rudeness, and not his obesity and baldness, caused women to turn away from him, never occured to him.

This very unhappy couple produced a child on whom they lavished all the material things their money could buy, but with no discipline and no regard for her feelings. She whined like her mother, she was rude like her father, and she tattled, taunted, belittled, and sneered like a caricature of a bratty child.

In a family session with the parents and Marilyn, the father said roughly to me, "When she's grown, she can buy a husband, and she can buy friends now. You tell her how."

"Nobody likes her," whined his wife, and her husband snarled at her, "Shut up! Nobody wants to hear what you have to say!"

With as much serenity as I could muster, I looked him in his baleful eye and said, "That was rude of you, and your daughter copies your rudeness. If the two of you want your daughter to learn some social skills, you will have to be more polite and considerate of each other as a model for her."

"My daughter," retorted Marilyn's father, "is worth two million dollars. She doesn't *need* social skills."

When last seen, Marilyn was being reluctantly dragged from the office by her indignant father, while her mother turned and looked at me with great admiration and whined, "You sure told him!"

Unfortunately, "telling him" had no effect, since the ultimate and regrettable result was that it caused him to withdraw his daughter from therapy. It is doubtful that either he or his wife ever changed. Marilyn may go through her entire life unliked, unwanted, and unhappy because of her parent's refusal to show consideration to each other or to other people. Hopefully, she will find a therapist when she is an adult who will help her learn to like other people and hence to be liked by them. Otherwise, the alternative is to buy herself "friends" and a husband as her father plans for her to do.

While this example is extreme, and while few parents believe their children can simply buy people like they can buy ice cream cones, it is not unusual for parents to teach their children rudeness, intolerance, and a lack of consideration for others by their behavior toward each other. If parents hit a child whenever they are angry, they can expect that child to hit other children; if parents are characteristically rude and discourteous to one another or to their children, they may expect their children to be rude to others; if parents withdraw and pout when things don't go their way, they should not be surprised when their children pout and sulk when they are thwarted.

There are other reasons why a child may behave with hostile aggression. In an older child, it usually signals frustration over helplessness in some important part of his life. A child may feel grief and despair over his parents' marital discord, for example, but feel helpless to do anything to change it. His frustration may then be expressed as hostile aggression. Or a child may feel inadequate in school and fear that he will fail in life. His fears may then be converted to rage at the world.

If your child is always angry and belligerent, your entire family needs help, because his anger is probably a symptom of some problem in the family. A family therapist can help you get the real trouble out so your child won't have to "take the rap" by being punished for his symptomatic aggressiveness. Until the basic problem is resolved, remove as much as possible all frustrating situations in his life, whether it is schoolwork that is too difficult for him, too many responsibilities at home, or too much criticism and punishment at home.

Since we're talking about aggression, let's define what we mean by the word. Would you rather your child be called "passive" or "aggressive?" Neither term is particularly appealing, because one usually calls up an image of a bland personality with all the spice of warmed-over oatmeal, while the other evokes images of hostility and violence.

It is not aggression that is a problem in children, but hostile violence or destruction that people label "aggression." Aggression is necessary and healthy; violence, hostility, and destructiveness are unnecessary and lead to inappropriate coping habits in a child that may remain with him for life.

For example, if Walter enters a track meet, that is aggressiveness. If Walter loses the race, and in his frustration begins throwing rocks at the winner, that is violence. One is healthy; the other is unhealthy and it is usually the unhealthy acts of hostile violence and destruction that parents and teachers refer to when they speak of "aggression."

Now, semantics aside, giving destructive behavior a proper label doesn't make it any less a problem when it exists. Whether the issue is a four-year-old who kicks his playmates, a six-year-old who roughly swings a kitten by its tail, a ten-year-old who stuffs lighted firecrackers through the mail slot of a neighbor's door, or a thirteen-year-old who cruelly bullies smaller children, the common denominator is senseless, violent destruction, and the important thing is to stop it.

Not surprisingly, the major cause of violence in children is violence in their parents. Parents who use belts or whips or wooden paddles to punish their children are not disciplinarians; they are child-beaters who are teaching their children to use violence to express anger. Parents who scream and curse at their children can expect their children to scream and curse at other children, and possibly to bully them or torment them as well. It cannot be stressed too often that children learn what they experience. If they experience kindness and fairness from their parents, with reasonable limits set on their behavior, they will treat others fairly and kindly, and will have inner controls on their own destructive impulses.

Children need to be taught from a very early age that anger is acceptable, but violence and destructiveness is not. By guiding children to properly direct anger in an acceptable, positive manner, they will learn to avoid violence.

The Influence Of Television

Next to parental models of violence, television is probably the most influential teacher. In study after study, it has been clearly demonstrated that children who watch as little as twenty minutes a day of "aggressive" television programs have less self-control than children who watch the same amount of nonviolent television programs. Children who mainly watch nonviolent television programs designed to provide models of social behavior, in fact, have greater self-control than do children who watch nonviolent, but neutral television shows.

When you consider that the average child from around

three years of age to about eighteen years spends more waking time in front of the television set than he spends anywhere else—including school—it's not surprising that television has a tremendous influence on his behavior and attitudes.

In the only government study of television's impact on children, the resulting report was prepared by five network officials and seven independent scientists. Reading like a Supreme Court decision in which none of the Justices concur, the report managed to say that televised violence both did and did not lead to greater violence in children. While some proponents of bloody carnage during the "family hour" maintain that it provides a healthy release of tension, it's impossible to ignore the government study's chilling conclusion that the best predictor of aggressive behavior at age nineteen is the amount of television violence watched in the third grade.

Anybody who's ever stood for a while and watched the newborn babies in a hospital nursery knows that some babies are born more aggressive than others. Some are angrily punching the air a few hours after birth, while others are contentedly sleeping. It stands to reason that a child who is more aggressive than the average may become overly aggressive if he is exposed to a lot of television violence and hostility in the home, especially if he isn't taught how to constructively express anger.

On the other hand, a child who has a highly tuned aggressive bent can be trained to be cooperative and constructively aggressive if he is provided with problem-solving models, and is surrounded by love and appropriate rewards and incentives.

There are certain times in a child's life when he will be more inclined toward aggression. Puberty in a boy may cause him to be more inclined to fight as the testosterone level in his blood increases. Adolescent girls may be more irritable just before their menstrual periods, and if they have been trained to get attention only through hostile behavior, they will intensify their irritation and be nasty and spiteful to members of their family, their classmates, and to everyone else. Boys and girls who have been trained to express hostility in appropriate ways, however, will be able to control their irritability during adolescence.

Whether your child was born placid or fighting, strictly limit the amount of violent TV shows and movies he views. While seeing violence on the screen doesn't compel a person to be violent, it certainly does increase the probability of violence in a person who is predisposed to hostile aggression, and it can teach inappropriate ways of expressing anger to those who aren't naturally aggressive.

Television is a powerful teaching tool, but unfortunately hasn't yet been used productively to alter antisocial behavior. To the contrary, it has too frequently been used thoughtlessly and irresponsibly and there's a strong probability that television has helped model antisocial behavior in frustrated and impressionable young people. Parents would do their children a great service, whether or not they show signs of antisocial hostility, by demanding more responsible television programming and by loudly voicing their protests over tasteless and senseless violence on TV. Until and unless the public is successful in changing some of the more irresponsible programming, it is the parents' responsibility to say "No" and keep the set turned off if a show is objectionable. In fact, a family game of Monopoly would probably be far more beneficial for everybody than *any* TV show!

You are the bows from which your children
as living arrows are sent forth.

-Kahlil Gibran,
The Report, 1923

Chapter Nine

SOMEBODY IS TEACHING THEM ABOUT SEX.
IS IT YOU?

Some time ago, I decided there might be questions about
sex that I was not adequately answering for the children
whom I see in play-therapy. Even though I am always careful
that every child I see receives factual information regarding
the human body and the process of reproduction, I thought
perhaps some of the children might have unanswered questions which they were too embarrassed or too shy to ask. So I
taped a sign saying "Sex Questions" to a cookie jar and asked
each child to please write on a piece of paper any questions he
or she might have about sex. I told each one that I would
write the answer and return the question to the cookie jar so
that all could read every question and every answer.

To a child, they looked at me blankly, briefly furrowed
their brows in futile thought, and then resumed their usual
play-therapy activities. Only one child managed to extract a
question from some recess in his mind, and I watched with
great curiosity as he laborously printed his question on a piece
of paper and deposited it in the cookie jar. Since he was the
first—and only—child to show any interest in my project, I
was quite anxious to see what he had written, and as soon as
his session ended and he was safely out of sight, I eagerly
dipped into the cookie jar and read his question.

It read: "WHY DO WE HAF TO WARE
UNNERWARE?"

After some thought, I answered, "I DON'T NO," and
retired the cookie jar back to its accustomed position of

holding modeling clay.

This incident highlighted a fact that we as adults usually forget, which is that children don't interpret the word "sex" they way adults do, and that their curiosity about sexual matters isn't an ongoing thing. Instead, it's stirred according to their own experiences and situations, and isn't necessarily in tune to adults' readiness to discuss it. Their curiosity is usually aroused when parents or other adults become embarrassed or try to avoid the issue when any questions come up regarding human bodies and their function, but by and large children are not terribly interested. If their questions are always answered in a matter-of-fact manner and if the changes in their bodies are explained to them as they take place, most children accept the place of sex in their lives as readily as they accept the place of bicycles or of homework.

Parents are the ones who find the subject of sex difficult to accept in an objective manner, because adults tend to think of "sex" as a euphemism for "sexual intercourse" and the very mention of the word "sex" causes them to experience whatever emotion they associate with their own sexual intimacy. They may be ashamed or aroused or embarrassed or frightened, but rarely do they accept sex as a child does—simply as another fact of life.

Parents also usually misunderstand a child's interest in sex as an interest in the mechanics of sexual intercourse. In actual fact, children are far more interested in understanding their own bodies than they are in knowing how adults make love. They want to know why girls can have babies and boys can't; they want to know why men have hair around their penises and why their penises are so large; they want to know what causes breasts to grow, and how milk gets in them when a woman has a baby; they want to know how a baby gets out of a mother; they want to know how it got in there in the first place; they want to know why they begin to smell bad when they are adolescents; they want to know about menstruation; they want to know about erections; they want to know about wet dreams; they want to know why grown-ups have hair under their arms; they want to know many things, but their interest is merely the interest of learning about their bodies and the world in which they live. There is no lascivious motivation, and no erotic curiosity. They want to know how babies are made in the same way in which they want to know how cars are made or how plants grow.

We have swung from a nation of prudes who "protected" our children from any knowledge of their own bodily functions or of reproduction to a nation whose people are almost feverish in their determination to lose their sexual inhibitions and to prevent any "sexual hang-ups" in growing children. Unfortunately, many parents create the "hang-ups" they want to avoid by going too far in the opposite direction and exposing their children to too much erotic sex too soon, in the mistaken belief that their children are curious about the erotic aspects of sex.

I know a mother, for example, who responded to her seven-year-old's question about how a baby began by sitting down with her and going through Alex Comfort's *The Joy of Sex*, explaining all the pleasures of sexual intercourse and oral-genital contact as if her seven-year-old needed or wanted that information. Rather than providing her child with needed information, she created sexual anxiety in the child which resulted in an anxious attempt to act out with her four-year-old brother all the pictures her mother had shown her. Her mother found her children's childish sexual acts amusing and healthy, and expressed delight that they were free of the "sexual hang-ups" she had as a child. The fact was, of course, that she still had severe "sexual hang-ups" which she was attempting to undo through her child, to the child's harm.

There are some families who stress nudity as a means of freeing their children of sexual repression. The usual reaction is not the casual acceptance of nudity as a normal state, as the parents hope, but a self-conscious attempt on the part of the children to respond to the parents' nudity in what they imagine is an adult manner, by ogling and poking. To be sure, if we lived in a society in which everybody was normally naked, nudity in the home would be totally commonplace, and would be taken for granted by the children. However, we live in a society in which people are normally clothed in public, and a display of nudity by parents therefore usually arouses curiosity and embarrassment in children. Once children reach school age they are usually slightly unsettled by the sight of their opposite-sex parents wandering about the house *sans* clothing. This is the age at which their own bodies are beginning to grow and change sexually, and they are acutely aware of the difference in their own bodies and those of their parents. They are also acutely aware of the fact that there is an element of exhibitionism in their parents' nude parades, and they are unsure how to respond to it.

This is not to say, of course, that the accidental sight of nude opposite-sex parents is harmful or that it should be rigidly avoided. If a little boy blunders into his mother's bathroom while she's in the tub there's no need for her to drown herself trying to cover her body. If a daughter walks into her parents' bedroom while her father is undressed, there's no need for dismay or alarm. But children will have a healthier sexual development if their opposite-sex parents keep bedroom and bathroom doors closed while they're undressed.

Nudity between a parent and child of the same sex, on the other hand, can be a very positive experience. A daughter may sit on the edge of the tub while her mother bathes, for example, and the two can hold long mother-daughter discussions about the age when breasts begin to grow, or when menstrual periods begin, or what causes vaginal itching or discharge.

Similarly, little boys can gain a good deal of information by talking with their nude fathers while they dress or shave. It makes no difference whether they talk about sports, sex, school, frogs, God, or girls. By studying his father's body, a boy can gain a clear knowledge of the future changes his own body will go through. At some point, fathers should mention the fact that their penises were small and insignificant when they were little boys, and that it is normal for testicles to move up and down with cold or excitement, and that it is normal for penises to be erect when a boy awakes in the morning, and that there is no bone inside a penis, and in general to discuss all the things they remember wondering about when they were boys.

Both parents should also discuss with their same-sex child the differences in the bodies of the opposite sex. Girls need a clear understanding of the workings of a boy's body, and boys need to understand that girls are not just boys without a penis. Each needs to understand the unique differences in the opposite sex so that they can avoid misunderstanding the behavior of the opposite sex when they begin dating.

Single parents with opposite-sex children needn't avoid sexual topics, but it is usually beneficial if a family friend or relative of the child's sex supplies part of a child's sex education if the only parent is of the opposite sex. Otherwise, there is a risk of sexual fantasy on the part of the child which can create guilt and anxiety.

A child's sexual experience begins the minute he is born, when he experiences the warmth and tactual pleasure of contact with his mother's body. Every fabric that touches his body, every scent he smells, every taste he experiences, and every sensation of touching with his fingers, toes, lips, and every other part of his body becomes a part of his sexual development. At some stage of his development in infancy, he will discover and touch his genitals, in the same manner in which he discovers and touches his toes. He will explore every part of his body with wonder and a sense of discovery, and this is a part of his sexual learning.

Throughout his infantile development, he will experience the pleasure of his body reacting to pleasant sensations such as the warm water in his bath, the smooth feel of talcum powder, the silkiness of his mother's hair, the roughness of his father's beard, the furry warmth of his stuffed toys, and the coolness of his crib sheets. He will enjoy the touch and smell of his parents' skin, the sensation of sucking and swallowing milk from his mother's breast or from a bottle, and the sound of wind chimes or of his music box. These too are elements in his developing sexuality.

When he is older, he will discover that there is a particularly pleasant sensation in his genital region when he rubs his hand there, and he may absently fondle his genitals as he falls asleep, or when he is tired or anxious. He thus learns the comforting sensation associated with sexuality.

When he is older still, he will begin to suspect that some other children have bodies that are not exactly like his, and he may anxiously try to see how their bodies are made because he will believe there is a possibility that there is something wrong with his. When he learns that boys have penises and girls have vaginas, that will seem totally unreasonable to him, and he and other children–who have the same suspicion that there is something about bodies they are not being told–may begin to check each other to make sure that indeed all girls have vaginas and all boys have penises. This is the age of "I'll show you mine if you'll show me yours" and of playing doctor. There is no feeling of erotic satisfaction as these children explore one another's bodies, but rather a kind of scientific curiosity which must be satisfied.

Parents frequently become outraged and anxious when they discover their children playing doctor or looking at one another's genital area. Sure they have produced a sexual deviant, they may punish or scold or humiliate a child discovered in such innocent play, and further create anxiety or suspicion in the child's mind that there is indeed something wrong with genitals. Rather than dampening his curiosity, punishment is more likely to cause more curiosity and can create a compulsive need to view undressed children.

When children are "caught with their pants down," parents would be wiser to simply tell them cheerfully to get dressed, and then help them find something else to do. Later, a parent can say, "I see that you are wondering how other people's bodies are made." A book with pictures of boys and girls in the nude, showing their penises and vaginas, is helpful to children at this age. Talking to them about the fact that *all* boys are made one way, and that *all* girls are made another way is reassuring. There is no reason to go into the reasons for the differences in a child of three or four, but a well-illustrated book such as *Where Do Babies Come From?* by Margaret Sheffield helps to answer many questions before they arise, and also helps parents overcome any shyness or embarrassment they may feel about discussing sex and reproduction with their children.

In selecting a book about reproduction, be very careful and mindful of the innate sensitivity of children. Children don't see the humor in sex, so stay away from the cutesy books which attempt to deal with sexuality as if it were a cartoon. Similarly, children are offended by cold, clinical details of sexual reproduction which treat human conception in the same manner as other animal conception. So don't try to evade the issue by buying your child a book that is mostly concerned with the reproduction of chickens or rabbits or cats, with humans added as just one other animal.

Children are basically honest and gentle little creatures who are entranced by the idea of their parents joining their bodies in love and creating a third person. Every child I see in therapy sits with me and listens as I read Sheffield's *Where Do Babies Come From?*, a book that is both factual and sensitive. Their reaction is usually one of quiet awe, and quite frequently they close the book with a satisfied sigh and say, "So my parents really *wanted* me!"

Just Answer The Questions

This is the age at which parents begin to be confronted with questions which they find difficult to answer. This is also the same time when parents set the stage for future communication with their children. Either their children will come to them with their problems and hopes and questions, or they will go to somebody else. Remember, when your child asks a question, don't recite the entire body of knowledge you have about sex, just answer the question.

For example, at one time or another your child will ask you or somebody else the following questions, and you or somebody else will hopefully provide the following answers:

Child: Mama, where did I come from?

Mother: You came from a special place inside my body.

Child: What special place?

Mother: A special place called a uterus, made just for babies to grow in.

Child: How did I get there?

Mother: You grew from a tiny, tiny egg in my body.

Child: Like a chicken?

Mother: Sort of like a chicken, except mother's eggs don't have shells. They're called ovum.

Child: How does the egg turn into a baby?

Mother: If a sperm from the Daddy meets one of the Mother's ovum, a baby will grow.

Child: What's a sperm?

Mother: Sperm are tiny, tiny things that sometimes come out of a Daddy's penis. If they go into the Mother's body and meet an ovum, a baby will begin to grow.

Child: How does the sperm get inside the Mother's body?

Mother: The Daddy puts his penis inside the Mother's vagina, and sperm goes into her body.

Child: How does the baby get out?

Mother: Through the vagina, the same way the sperm went into her body.

Child: Did you and Daddy do that?

Mother: Yes, we loved each other and wanted a baby, and that's how we got you.

Child: Will I have a baby?

Mother: If you want to, you probably will.

As you can see, this conversation could be ended at any time, with the child's questions thoroughly answered. So long as a child continues to ask questions, the parent should continue to answer honestly and directly, but providing only an answer to the question asked, and not elaborating on the answer unless the child seems to need elaboration.

Once you have survived such a round of questioning, don't think you can breathe a sigh of relief and put it behind you forever. It will come up again and again, until the questions and answers almost take on a ritualistic quality, like a bedtime story. As your children grow older, their questions will become more personal, and if they become more personal than you can comfortably answer, it's best to honestly say that you don't like to talk about your own sex life but that you'll answer general questions honestly. If your child asks a question that you don't know the answer to, say that you don't know, and try to find the answer at the library.

Remember too, that children don't save their questions about sex for a quiet, private time when just you and they are together. Instead, they ask questions about sex while you stand in line at the supermarket, or when you're having a hamburger at McDonald's, or while you're visiting your maiden aunt who never had a date. If the timing is inappropriate, gently tell your child that you will give her the answer later, and be sure to keep your promise without scolding her for being indiscreet in asking. *Every* question, no matter how explicit, should be answered.

As your child gets older, he will ask more difficult questions. Some of the toughies, and their answers, are:

Child: What is a prostitute?

Parent: A prostitute is a person who has sexual intercourse for money.

Child: What is a queer/faggot/lezzie?

Parent: Some people call homosexuals "queer" or "faggot" or "lezzie", but usually most kids use those words to insult each other, like calling somebody a dog.

Child: What's a homosexual?

Parent: A homosexual is a grown-up person who has a choice and chooses his or her own sex to have sexual intercourse with. (It is very important to make the distinction of *grown up* when discussing homosexuality with children, since most young pepole form emotional attachments to same-sexed peers, and many youngsters feel some sort of sexual response to members of their own sex. If they label themselves "queer" because of this, they may live up to the label long after they have outgrown this homosexual phase of their development. Boys, especially, may engage in mutual or parallel masturbation during their preadolescent or adolescent years, and if they are discovered and labeled homosexual because of it, they may believe they truly are homosexual.)

Child: What is rape?

Parent: Rape is when a man forces a woman to have sexual intercourse when she doesn't want to.

Child: What is a wet dream?

Parent: A wet dream is what boys begin to have when they are about thirteen years old and some semen comes out of their penis while they are asleep. Semen looks like white lotion, and about a tablespoon comes out during a wet dream. A wet dream shows that a boy is growing up.

Child: What's a period?

Parent: A period is what girls call their menstrual period, when a little blood and fluid from their uterus comes out their vagina.

Child: Why does it do that?

Parent: Because it isn't needed to nourish a baby. From the time a girl is about thirteen years old, her body gets ready for a baby to begin every month. The lining of her uterus starts getting thicker with blood, and if a baby began it would get its nourishment there. If there is no baby, the blood isn't needed, and it is discharged along with a lot of watery fluid through the vagina. Menstruation shows that a girl is growing up.

Child: What's a vagina?

Parent: A vagina is sort of like a hollow tube that can stretch very large so a baby can come through.

Child: Where is it?

Parent: It's connected to a woman's uterus at one end and the other end is right below the place where a woman urinates.

Child: How do people have intercourse?

Parent: A man puts his penis in a woman's vagina and moves it back and forth.

Child: Does it feel good?

Parent: If both people want to do that, it usually feels good.

Child: What are balls?

Parents: Balls are what people call testicles and they hang under a man's penis.

Child: What are they for?

Parent: Testicles are where sperm are made. Sperm can't live in very warm temperature, so testicles hang in a little pouch outside the man's body where it's a little cooler.

As you can see, you must have factual information in order to answer all your child's questions. If you got *your* sex education in the same place that most people did—on the school ground or in the school restroom—then be sure that you have read and learned accurate sex information long before your child asks questions, so you'll be ready before the questions begin.

What Do You Feel About Masturbation?

Many times, having the information and feeling comfortable imparting it to one's own child are two very different things. Once at a seminar for professionals who dealt with human sexual dysfunction, the keynote speaker gave a telling demonstration of the difficulty parents frequently have in dealing with their own children's sex education.

First, he asked how many of us believed that masturbation was a normal, healthy sexual activity. All the professionals present raised their hands. Next, he asked how many of us were parents. The majority of the audience raised their hands. And finally, he asked how many of us, professionals who were knowledgable and sophisticated regarding masturbation, had instructed our children in *how* to masturbate. I doubt that there was a person present who didn't feel shocked and offended.

In our society, masturbation is strictly a personal matter, and even those whose professions focus on human sexuality rarely instruct another person in masturbation. There are some primitive societies in which mothers instruct and assist their children in masturbation, but that idea is shocking and distasteful to most "civilized" societies.

It's little wonder that many parents are unsure about what their response should be toward their children's masturbation. It's difficult for a parent to know when a child's masturbation is a normal activity or when it's a signal of excessive tension or anxiety, and what to do about it in either case.

Generally speaking, toddlers who rub their genitals are doing so because it gives them pleasure. If it is very frequent, they may be comforting themselves because of boredom or anxiety or because of some infection which causes a genital itching. If the behavior is almost continuous, a physical exam to rule out infection should be the parents' first response, since urinary-tract infections or allergies to soap, bubble bath—a frequent offender—or food may be the problem.

If no infection or allergy is present, but a toddler prefers to masturbate rather than to play with other children or with toys, the next focus should be on the amount of tension in the home. Are the parents constantly scolding and saying, "No?" Is there a great deal of arguing and bickering between the parents? Is there unhappiness in the home? If the answer to any of these questions is "Yes," then tension is probably causing the child to need the comfort of continually handling his genitals.

Even in an emotional climate that is serene, a child may masturbate out of boredom, and may need more intellectual or social stimulation. Don't forget, however, that children from the happiest, most stress-free homes, with adequate intellectual stimulation and love, will handle their genitals often, simply because it gives them pleasure. There is nothing immoral or abnormal about it. It is only when such behavior is continuous and compulsive, or when it is always *preferred* to playing with stimulating toys that it indicates underlying tension and anxiety.

Open and continuous masturbation in non-retarded schoolage children is almost always related to tension. Anxious first or second graders, for example, may absently rub their genitals as they do seatwork or listen to their teacher. Again, when the tension at home or at school is lifted, the compulsive masturbation usually stops. If it doesn't and there's no infection or anatomical abnormality, it indicates a compulsive need to relieve tension and anxiety, and professional help should be sought to find the underlying cause.

Many parents who feel guilty about masturbating themselves become angry and anxious when they see their children masturbating. If your toddler is masturbating in a normal manner, just before going to sleep, when she is bored or ill, or when she is anxious, and you feel an irrational anger or anxiety about it, check your attitudes about your own masturbation and get clear with yourself about what is normal and what is abnormal before you become alarmed about your child. Forget all the silly stories you ever heard about how masturbation will make a person "go crazy." Masturbation won't make a person do anything except feel better.

The idiotic notion that masturbation causes insanity stems from the fact that some psychotics in mental hospitals have so completely lost contact with reality and with their surroundings that they may openly masturbate in the same way a toddler does. Rather than recognizing the fact that the mental illness led to the open and continuous masturbation, misguided observers jumped to the erroneous conclusion that masturbation had caused the insanity. That's like believing that bleeding causes a knife wound, but there are still some people who hold these and equally stupid beliefs.

Also, forget the idea that *some* masturbation is normal, but that *excessive* masturbation is abnormal. People who hold this belief will judge the amount of masturbation *they* do as *some*, and any more than that as *excessive*. Children, like adults, masturbate as much or as little as they need to. One child may need the comfort and pleasure of masturbation every day, while another may need it once a week, and still another may need it several times a day. In school-age children, unless masturbation is compulsive, and preferred to all other activity that is available, and done without regard to the presence of other people, it is not abnormal and there is nothing to worry about. Even when there is absent-minded, compulsive and continuous masturbation in public, there may be some infection or allergy causing persistent itching, and what appears to be masturbation may actually be scratching. A good physical examination should be the first reaction. And if there are no physical problems, look to the emotional climate in the home. If there are no obvious problems in the marriage or in the family, an appointment with a family therapist, child psychologist, or child psychiatrist might be in order.

If Children Are Sexually Abused

This discussion about children and sex isn't complete without mention of a very unpleasant subject. Sexual abuse of children is something none of us likes to think about, but something which every parent must be prepared for. Cases of sexual abuse of children are much more frequent than most people realize, simply because they so often go unreported or unprosecuted. The rationale in many cases is that the trauma for a child of openly accusing their abusers in court and experiencing the questioning and remembering which would accompany criminal prosecution is potentially more harmful to the child than letting the child abuser go free. A more significant reason for the failure of sex abusers of children to be prosecuted and punished is that the offenders are very frequently parents or parent substitutes or some other relative or close family friend, and the sexual abuse is never reported.

A typical situation of sexual abuse of a child is one in

which a woman with young children marries a man who is immature, impulsive, and demanding. If he is left alone for long periods of time with a young stepdaughter, and if he is a heavy drinker or drug user, and if the sexual relationship between him and his wife is unsatisfactory, he may become aroused by his stepdaughter. Given sufficient time and a sufficient loss of inhibitions through alcohol or drug consumption, he may fondle her gently, causing her innocent pleasure. Encouraged by her pleasure, he may instruct her in caressing his genitals, and if she complies with no fear, he may gradually progress to more intimate contact such as inserting his finger in her vagina or performing cunnilingus on her. If he loses all control, he may penetrate her vagina with his penis.

If he is sufficiently gradual in his approach so that the child is not frightened, and if she receives little or no affection from her mother or other relatives, there may develop an incestuous relationship which can last for years before the child begins to have feelings of guilt when she realizes their activity is held immoral by society.

In many cases, the child's mother unconsciously or consciously promotes the activity because of sexual problems of her own. When it is forcefully brought to her attention, she may react as if her daughter were her rival and reject her. In many cases, the mother had incestuous relations as a child with someone in her own family. Like her daughter, she may have found affection only through sexual behavior.

In these situations, the trauma to the child is magnified because of the mother's encouragement of the incestuous relationship. Women who were sexually molested by fathers or stepfathers as children seem to have more difficulty resolving their hatred and resentment toward their mothers for permitting them to be used than they hold toward the man who used them.

Many times children will remain silent when a relative attempts to sexually molest them because they believe they will be punished if they tell their parents. Unfortunately, their belief is often realistic. Parents frequently brand a child a liar

175

if she tells them a grandparent or uncle or family friend has made sexual overtures. The child is thus left with the trauma of the experience itself plus the trauma of her parents' disloyalty and disbelief.

The stereotype of a sex offender against children is that of a "weird" man of subnormal intelligence who is easily recognized. The fact is that he may be an intelligent man holding a responsible position and appearing to all the world as sexually normal. The factor that sets a child molester apart from other men is not his intelligence or religious beliefs, but some defect in thinking or reasoning that causes him to see children as very small people with the same motives, ideas, and intentions as large people.

Thus, a man with this kind of defect in his ability to see children as children may be perfectly normal in every other respect, but if a three-year-old sits in his lap and squirms in a way that stimulates his genitals, he will sincerely believe that the child is being deliberately provocative, and that his sexual response is thoroughly known and understood by the child. If he is alone with the child, he may respond by fondling her genitals, and if he is someone the child knows and trusts, she may accept the fondling as a pleasurable form of affection, and lean back against him contentedly. The progression toward sexual abuse will then be almost inevitable, since the man will interpet her every action as deliberate and sexually knowledgeable.

If the man's behavior becomes known and he is confronted by angry parents or by child welfare authorities, a man with this kind of personality defect will rarely feel ashamed or guilty. Instead, he will be sorry his behavior was found out, and he may very likely feel self-righteously bitter. Many such men believe they have been betrayed by a three- or four-year-old child who seduced them and then told her parents and got them into trouble!

So, without becoming paranoid and distrustful of your best friends, be aware that there are people in the world who for some reason do not understand the distinction between children and adults and who will sexually exploit your children. Pay close attention to nonverbal cues your children may send out which can alert you to something amiss in their relationship with an adult. If your child seems to avoid a particular adult's company, for instance, and if that adult seems to inordinately seek him or her out, pay close attention. Be aware that sexual molesters of children may be women as well as men, and that little boys are molested as well as little girls. If your child complains that a certain adult "touches" them too much, or that an adult "tickles them in the wrong place," pay attention.

By the same token, pay attention if your child seems sexually provocative. If your three-year-old decides to join a party of adults wearing nothing but her happiest smile, there is nothing particularly noteworthy about it, and an appropriate response on your part would be to cheerfully lead her to her room and put clothes on her. If a seven-year-old does the same thing, however, there is a problem which should be handled by a professional.

Many parents seem to promote sexual precocity in their children because of their own sexual boredom. A mother whose life is boring and lacking in excitement may unconsciously push her daughter to dress and behave provocatively so that she can vicariously enjoy her daughter's resulting sexual popularity. The current women's fashions, which seem to be copies of clothing worn in the bordellos of the 30's, are appropriate on a young woman of twenty-three on a disco dance floor because she and the other young people there understand the language of the clothing. It allows them to play a role without revealing anything about themselves, and they can therefore throw themselves into the dances with wild abandon while maintaining the illusion of anonymity because of their costumes.

The same clothing, however, is frequently worn by young girls in junior high school and elementary school, because their mothers enjoy the vicarious thrill of exhibitionism. When an immature adult male with an inability to use appropriate judgment sees a young girl dressed like a pint-sized hooker, he takes her at face value and will act accordingly. The result may not be the fun and excitement the girl and her mother felt when they chose the clothing, but tragedy and pain.

In spite of the best of parental guidance and the most scrupulous family care, some children are sexually molested and they and their parents must deal with the unfortunate incident in a manner that will leave the fewest emotional scars for the child. If your child should have the bad luck to be sexually molested, let your first consideration be to comfort her and to reassure her that she has done no wrong. Don't make the mistake of questioning her in a way that will make her feel she is responsible or at fault. It does no good and a lot of harm to demand, "What were you doing talking to a stranger?" or similar questions.

Comfort and calm her to the best of your ability, and try to maintain your own calm. Unless there is actual physical injury, the incident can be simply an unpleasant experience which your child can absorb and leave behind if you remain calm and comforting. If she has been fondled or if a man has exposed his genitals to her, or if there has been an attempted rape with some physical struggle, talk to her quietly and tell her that some people are sick and confused and that her fear is understandable and that she did well to fight or to come and tell you about it. If a similar incident happened to you in your childhood, tell her about it and tell her that you understand the fear and confusion she felt.

After you have calmed her and comforted her, deal with the situation as best you can. If the molester is known to you, there should be a report to the police. If there was actual rape and physical damage to your child, comfort her and get medical help as speedily as possible. Treat the physical injury as you would treat any other injury, and comfort your child in the same manner that you would comfort her if she had been attacked and struck on the face or body. Don't let the fact that the attack was a sexual one cause you or your child to feel any humiliation or shame, and be very sure that your child is not made to feel responsible for her pain. Avoid like the plague the pseudo-psychologists who will try to convince you that some unconscious fears of your own *caused* her to be raped, and avoid the religious zealot who will try to convince you that your child's rape was punishment for some sexual sin of your own.

Stay as calm as possible and stay with your child and comfort and reassure her as much as possible. And do not, when the pain and trauma have gone away, decide to let the rapist go free. Your child needs to know that you and she do not allow violations to go unpunished, and if the courtroom is not filled with histrionics or overly emotional charges, it can be a valuable experience in asserting her rights as an individual. Most important, it can save another child from the same experience if the rapist is convicted and confined to prison.

Psychotherapy may be needed to help a child victim of rape or molestation completely erase the emotional scars and be able to go on to a normal sex life as an adult. If your child should be unfortunate enough to experience a rape, don't delay in getting professional help for her and for yourself.

Don't Be Dumb About Sex Education

Remember that there is little probability of unpleasant or damaging sexual experiences for your child, and that your main concern is to help him or her grow up with healthy and responsible sexual feelings. You can best do that by giving your child lots of physical affection, thereby providing the touching satisfaction that is a basic need of every human being. Babies who are not touched often enough, in fact, don't thrive and grow as well as babies who receive lots of cuddling and touching. In studies involving infant monkeys, who have similar touching needs, researchers found that monkeys raised without mothers but with other baby monkeys to snuggle next to grew up with more social and sexual health than monkeys who were raised with their mothers but without other baby monkeys to play with. The researchers concluded that the physical contact was more important to normal social and sexual development than the presence of a mother was, since the mothers didn't spend as much time touching the baby monkeys as the babies spent touching each other.

Children who are not touched and hugged and patted and kissed and cuddled are apt to grow up with such strong needs for that kind of contact that they may initiate sexual contact in order to be touched. Many sexually promiscuous people are not driven by a need for sex, in fact, but by a need to be hugged and physically close to another person. So to help your child associate mature love with physical closeness, be sure that you give him lots of hugs and approving pats. He will not only grow up with more self-esteem and self-confidence, but he will be more likely as an adult to use sexual activity as a means of expressing affection than to use sex as a means of obtaining physical contact without affection.

Someday, perhaps we as a society will have matured to the point that children are taught about their bodies in school and at home with the same degree of accuracy and objectivity that we use when we teach them about the ocean or the stars. To behave as if some parts of the human body are dirty and sinful and not to be talked about is to invite a sense of guilt and anxiety which will pervade every aspect of a child's personality. As an adolescent, a child who has been taught by word and implication that normal bodily functions are nasty and degrading will have difficulty relating to members of the opposite sex as individuals. Instead, such a child will relate to them as either objects to be exploited and used for forbidden sexual pleasures or as threatening seducers who must be fearfully avoided.

It is a fallacy that factual information regarding sex will lead children to experimentation and early sexual intercourse. Our sex-saturated movies, television shows, and billboard advertising are probably contributing to earlier sexual experimentation between youngsters, but there is a vast difference between titillating scenes of sexual behavior among adults and objective, factual information designed to eliminate the harmful myths and untruths regarding sexuality.

More than a million teen-aged girls become pregnant every year in the United States. Our country has the sad distinction of having a higher percentage of teen-aged pregnancies than Japan, Sweden, West Germany, Israel, Norway, France, Russia, and 14 other countries! Although teen-aged women account for only 18% of sexually active females in the United States, they account for 46% of all illegitimate births and 31% of all abortions. The staggering fact is that there are 200,000 illegitimate births to teenagers every year, and 300,000 abortions among teenagers. About 100,000 other girls hastily marry after they become pregnant and have legitimate births.

These are not necessarily first-time illegitimate births. Sometimes they are a girl's second, third, or even fourth pregnancy before the age of fifteen. Even more mind-boggling is the fact that 32 twelve-year-old girls gave birth to babies in California in 1974!

Clearly, we are doing something wrong, and the something wrong appears to be flooding the media with the provocative idea that sex is always fun and satisfying, without providing information that will enable young people to approach sex with factual knowledge and a sense of responsibility.

Even sexually experienced adults are confused by much of the hype regarding sex. Seeing the idealized fantasy of instant, earthshaking, orgasmic thrills on the movie screen, the average adult looks with furtive jealousy at the other movie-goers, thinking they all must have such fantastic sex, and feeling inadequate and abnormal. Teenagers are likely to have complete faith in the movie version of sex, and become determined to experience what appears to be an ultimate pleasure attainable by simply meeting the right person.

If we are to help children develop healthy sexual attitudes and responsible sexual behavior, we must guard against too much exposure to erotic sex and also against too much repression of normal sexual curiosity. All of the studies of people who engage in deviant sexual behavior point to the fact that too much repression of normal sexual curiosity is likely to lead to sexual deviancy in later life. It has been found that rapists and people who sexually molest children, for example, were less likely in childhood to have masturbated, to have seen any pornographic material, to have seen any nudity in their homes, or to have received any information about sex from their parents.

On the other hand, too much erotic sexual openness between adults in the home can be detrimental to a child's sexual development because it excites their own sexual imagination and causes them to imagine sexual contact with their opposite-sex parent. These feelings then lead to guilt feelings, feelings of worthlessness, feelings of fear because children believe in instant retribution for their "bad" feelings, and to feelings of resentment toward their parents for creating the situation that lead to their taboo feelings.

If your child should accidently witness you and your spouse having sexual intercourse, she is not likely to be permanently traumatized unless you act with undue rage or humiliation. If you treat the incident with honesty and tact, the incident can be one that your child can remember with warmth and confidence.

However, if you are *always* careless about leaving your bedroom door unlocked, or if you have a habit of impulsively making love on the living room sofa or dining room floor while your children are in the house, then you probably have some unconscious exhibitionistic tendencies which make you *want* to be seen by your children. To avoid giving your children feelings of vague guilt, anxiety, confusion, and possible future sexual problems, keep your sex life private and out of sight. If you find this impossible to do, it would be wise for you to seek some professional counseling to find out why you need a childish audience in order to enjoy sex.

The best sex education for any child is to have loving parents who enjoy their sex life together and who are moderately public about it. Seeing Mom and Dad lovingly kissing each other is something that gives children a sense of security and comfort. Seeing Dad give Mom a playful pat on the fanny, or vice versa, teaches them that there is an element of fun in sex. Seeing both parents keep themselves attractive and good-smelling for one another teaches them that maintaining a satisfactory sexual relationship takes some effort and consideration, and seeing them go off for the weekend together or retreat to their bedroom and lock their bedroom door teaches them that a satisfactory sexual relationship is something that deserves quality time and attention.

Since parents such as these are usually confident and relaxed about their sex life–neither giving it exaggerated importance nor treating it as if it were something that needed no attention–they will usually answer their children's questions honestly and factually, and the children are less likely to need to engage in experimental behavior or to become prematurely sexually active in order to satisfy their sexual curiosity.

If you handle sexuality with your children with common sense and dignity, being neither too uninhibited or too repressive, you can guide them toward responsible and pleasurable sexuality as adults. Answer their questions with honesty and factual information, warn them without alarming them about people who may take advantage of them sexually, teach them how to dress and behave so they don't inadvertantly attract the attention of sexual deviants who might harm them, let them observe some manifestations of your sexuality without being exhibitionistic or seductive, and help them accept their own sexuality as a normal and worthy part of themselves. Don't push them toward sexual attitudes or behavior before they're ready, and don't try to hold them back from normal and appropriate responses when they are ready. Above all, work at developing a sex life for yourself that is pleasurable, responsible, private, and totally fulfilling so that you will not foist on your children any sexual frustrations or sexual fears that belong to you. If your sex life is frustrating, unrewarding, or unpleasant, get professional help for yourself and you will be helping to ensure that your child will have healthier attitudes toward sex.

Children are unpredictable.
You never know what inconsistency
they're going to catch you in next.
-Franklin P. Jones

Chapter Ten

EVEN IF THE MARRIAGE DISSOLVES, THE FAMILY CONTINUES

While the purpose of this book is to offer some encouragement and possible help in dealing with the problems that every family encounters in one form or another, there is one situation which is not common to every parent, but it touches the lives of all of us. Today's divorce rate is so high that it seems surprising that 68% of all children in the United States are living with both natural parents. Many of these intact homes will dissolve, however, and 19% of all children in this country currently live in one-parent households. For many, the one-parent arrangement is temporary, as most divorced parents eventually remarry. About 10% of all children live with a natural parent and a stepparent. (The remaining 3% live with relatives, foster parents, or in institutions.) By 1990 the prediction is that probably more than half of all children in the United States will have lived for a while in a one-parent household.

Some children divide their time equally between divorced parents in a joint-custody arrangement, but most see their non-custodial parent only on weekends. Some never see the non-custodial parent after the divorce, nor receive any financial support from him or her.

Divorce when a child is involved is always a distressing event. For the parents, divorce may release them from a commitment made when they were too young or too inexperienced to make a lasting decision. If the relationship was destructive and constricting, divorce may allow them to

185

rebuild their lives and assert their personalities in positive, fulfilling ways. If they married before they were fully grown up, divorce may allow parents to finally realize themselves and to follow whatever paths their needs demand.

For children, however, divorce simply means that something is amiss in their world. Almost all children have an instinctive feeling that parents are an indissoluble unit which neither divorce nor death changes. For that unit to split is traumatic to a child because it is contrary to his perception of the natural order of things. While a child may feel more relaxed and calm when the tension of an unhappy marriage is removed, he will still feel a sense of profound loss and uneasiness because of the change in the family.

This is not to say that children are irreparably harmed by divorce. A child whose parents are unhappy and who is damaged by uncompromising clashes over basic philosophies and needs may be more traumatized by the distressful family situation than he would be by a peaceful divorce. Happy parents are the best insurance for a child of well-adjusted development, and if the parents are happy divorced but miserable married, divorce is probably the lesser of two evils.

When I have my power fantasies of deciding for the world how it should be run, I sometimes imagine a world in which nobody could marry or conceive children until they were at least thirty years old and had fully developed as people, sure of what and who they were and what they wanted and needed for their own happiness and fulfillment. If that were the case, there would be far fewer divorces and fewer children hurt by the dissolution of their families.

In my fantasies, however, I can never imagine a nation of over-thirty men and women being willing to give up their satisfying, rewarding lives and take on twenty-year commitments of raising children, especially when the current estimated cost of raising a child to the age of eighteen is in excess of $254,000! To be sure, there would be many people who would welcome the opportunity to live with children and help them develop and grow perfectly, but a lot of others would be reluctant to lose their total freedom by having families.

Having babies when you're not old enough and wise enough to know what a demanding responsibility you've taken on is probably like volunteering to fight in a war when you're so young that you believe wars are like television shows or movies. We probably owe our very existence to the rash faith with which young people enter into life's most important and demanding situations.

So, in spite of my imagined Utopian world in which every baby is wanted and every parent is a mature, fulfilled parent, and in which every marriage is one the partners *want* but don't *need*, I suppose we are stuck with the system we have. Men and women will continue to fall in love and marry and then sometimes fall out of love and divorce when they have already had children, and the children will pay the greatest price.

How Divorce Affects Kids

If your child is under the age of four when you divorce, he will be less damaged than he will be after he is old enough to have a better developed sense of social standards. Under four years, he will still accept with self-centered pleasure or pain the fact that people important in his world come and go. But he won't add to his uneasiness by knowing that *most* children have two parents living together when one parent moves from his home.

The most important consideration for the younger child of divorced parents is that his life and routine remain fairly consistent. To have regular mealtimes and bedtimes with one parent and then to have a very irregular schedule with the other parent on weekends usually causes fatigue and crankiness in very young children.

When this happens, the parent with custody usually has to live with a whiney child for several days until his schedule and sense of security has returned. Sometimes, when there is continuing animosity and feelings of revenge between parents, the situation will become one in which the weekend parent deliberately may sabotage the tranquility of the custodial parent's home in the immature belief that he or she is "punishing" the other parent. The person being punished, of course, is the child.

Older children have an acute sense of disaster when their parents divorce. Very often, they don't actually know the meaning of the word "divorce" but they know it spells trouble for a family. Children have to be reassured that parents divorce each other but not their children, and that divorce doesn't mean they'll have a different father or different mother.

For a time after a divorce, children usually feel intense guilt or anger or fear, and their feelings must be allowed full expression. They may be angry at their mother for forcing or allowing their father to leave. They may be angry at their father for not staying with their mother. They may feel responsible for the divorce and believe it's because of their own bad behavior. They may believe they will never see the absent parent again.

It's best if parents can sit down together with their children when they have absolutely decided to divorce and talk to them as calmly and rationally as possible about their decision. Without blaming one another and without going into details, they should honestly tell their children that they're not happy living together, and that they've decided to live in separate houses. They should assure their children of their continual love, and explain their plans for the children to spend time with the parent who is moving out.

It's often helpful for the children to visit their leaving-parent's new home or apartment before he actually moves. It's especially important for the parent setting up a new home to set aside a special room or nook reserved solely for the child. A knowledge that he has a room and bed and furniture which belongs to him in his other parent's home helps a child feel secure in the knowledge that his relationship with that parent will continue after the divorce.

If possible, it's best to have duplicate clothing and toys at the new home-away-from-home, so there's no need to pack a bag on weekends as if he's visiting a stranger. Having his own toothbrush, his own pajamas and his own bike at both homes aids a child in feeling secure, and helps his world have a continuity which is important.

An ideal arrangement, of course, would be for the child to remain in his own home, and for the parents to move in and out, taking turns living in the house. In that way, the child's world remains the same, with the same familiar surroundings and friends and only the parent-figure changes.

Sometimes parents are able to manage that kind of cooperation, either for a short transitional period or for a longer period of time, but eventually there will be a need for each parent to have his or her own home. If the parents can arrange to have their respective homes within the same school zone, or in the same general neighborhood, a child can visit each parent at will and spend the night or have dinner with the non-custodial parent without interrupting his regular routine too much.

Frequently and irrationally, the non-custodial parent will become paranoid and suspicious if the custodial parent asks him to keep the child for an evening or overnight when the time is not one of his "ordered" visitation times. Forgetting that the child is a joint responsibility, he may righteously declare, "I'm not going to babysit for you!"

Since the custodial parent "babysits" for the absent parent regularly, that reasoning seems particularly cloudy. Such irrational behavior on the part of a divorced parent isn't uncommon, however, and many divorced parents continue to keep their old relationship alive by finding things to fight about. They may fight over the time of visitation, with the custodial parent counting every second the child spends with the noncustodial parent beyond the court decreed time. Or they may fight over child support, with the non-custodial parent delaying sending his share of his child's support every month so that the mother is anxious and angry. Or he may withhold the money entirely in order to force the mother into a battle in the unconscious wish to keep some sort of relationship with her going, even if it is an unpleasant one. By using their children as pawns, some parents battle each other after divorce as they did before divorce, thereby keeping a sick relationship alive and at the same time destroying the emotional health of their children, who are usually forced to "take sides."

Whether a divorced parent's manner of continuing a relationship with her ex-spouse is to demand split-second adherence to the visitation hours set by the court or whether it is a parent's failure to share in the financial responsibility of parenthood, the behavior is immature and unbecoming and sets poor examples for their children. It's bad enough for a child to have parents who must divorce, but it's even worse to have parents who can't make a success of their divorce any more than they could make a success of their marriage.

If your marriage is or has become unworkable, let your divorce be clean and honorable, without dirty infighting and hostile skirmishes involving the children. Share in the responsibility of parenting even if you can't share anything else, and never forget that neither of you "gets" the children, regardless of who has custody. Children belong to themselves and they are not pets to be fought over.

Integrating Their New Lives

One of the things you must remember when or if you get a divorce is that your child has the task of integrating into his life the two new lives which you and your divorced partner have. While you may wish to completely remove your ex-spouse from your life, your child can't do that and still remain the person he is–a child with two parents–and it is vitally important that you allow him to assimilate his two worlds in his own way.

A child's way of assimilating and integrating the two worlds into which divorce thrusts him is to talk to one parent about the other. If you're a divorced mother, your child may tell you about his father's new apartment and how nifty it is and how his father got a huge new color TV set and how there is a magnificent pool at his apartment where beautiful young girls sun themselves and how his father just bought a new red Porche.

If you feel your temperature rising, as you steer your five-year-old station wagon with the slick tires toward your own home where the TV set with the burned-out tube sits waiting for you to get the necessary money to have it repaired, cool it. What you don't know is that your child is telling his father how you got a new expensive permanent and how you forgot to lock the front door one night and how you went out to dinner with a man who had a huge gold ring and who brought you roses and how you usually feed him canned soup for dinner now because you're so busy learning to disco dance that you don't have time to cook.

All of these things may have some element of truth in them, and some may be total fabrications from his imagination, but they are all designed to do one of two things. Conseiously or unconsciously your child may be attempting to keep you and your ex-husband united in the way he remembers you–angry and resentful–or he may simply be trying to keep each of you alive when he is with the other, so that he retains his feeling of an intact family.

Remember that his interpretation of his own statements might be a great deal different than your interpretation is. He may be trying to communicate to both of you, "Listen, even though you don't want to live with each other any more, and even though you make each other unhappy, I am aware that you still love each other a little and that you still wonder about each other. I'll act as messenger for both of you, and let you know how well the other is doing so you won't worry. I won't tell you how sad Dad looks because it might make you feel guilty. And I won't tell you how sad it makes me feel when I see the picture of all of us in his bedroom. Instead, I'll tell you all the things I think will make you feel better. I'll exaggerate a little bit about the size of the TV set, and I'll make everything else sound a little more glamorous than it really is so you won't worry about Dad."

And to his father he may be saying, "Don't worry about Mom. She's trying to build a new life and she's doing a pretty good job. She's sad a lot and worried about money, but she's doing the best she can, and I'm proud of how pretty she is, and I want you to know that other people think she's pretty, too."

On the other hand, he may tell you how his father spent the entire weekend drinking beer and watching television, and he may tell his father that you're never home anymore and that he has to heat his own TV dinners. In this way, he may be trying to communicate, "I want you back together. If I make you mad enough at each other because you're worried about me, maybe you'll get into a fight and fall in love again."

As much as possible, grit your teeth and smile when your child talks about how well his other parent is doing, or about how neglectful his other parent is. Try to keep the lines of communication open so that you can talk to the other parent about things you find particularly stressful, but keep your sense of humor about the entire situation. Unless your ex-spouse is hopelessly irresponsible and hopelessly unkind, your child is undoubtedly treated well at his other home.

The need which children have to integrate all the people in their world is particularly important to bear in mind when and if stepparents enter the scene. Invariably, your child will zero in on the skills and abilities which you don't have and which the stepparent does. He doesn't do this to make you jealous or because he's losing loyalty to you, he does it to share with you the fact that his world has been expanded by the addition of a stepparent. He is trying to be pleased about it, even though he's not. He's also trying in his own way to adjust to the fact that a stepparent means true finality of his parents' divorce. In his childish way, he is trying to swallow his disappointment and make the best of the situation.

He expects you to be pleased by that, since he doesn't

understand the irrational jealousies and insecurities most adults have. And he will be hurt and confused if you react with less than pleasure when he extols the virtues of his new stepmother or stepfather.

If you're a so-so cook, he will tell you about the delicious meals his new stepparent prepares. If you are a clumsy carpenter, he will tell you how his new stepparent single-handedly built an architectural wonder in his back yard. If you are a home-body who enjoys a quiet evening with a good book and a glowing fireplace, he will tell you what a life-of-the-party his new stepparent is, and how glamorous she is as she goes out on the town.

Take all these integrating expressions of admiration from your child with good grace and good humor. *Don't* snap at him, "I'm not interested!" He won't understand that, and it will cause him to have to compartmentalize his various worlds, something that is painful for him. Try to be grown up enough to listen to somebody else's virtues, even if the somebody else is one whom you suspect broke up your marriage, without feeling resentful and jealous. At least, take pleasure in the fact that your child is happy with his new stepparent.

While it may seem that the number of men who retain custody of their children is increasing, a la *Krammer vs. Krammer*, the fact is that the *percentage* of custodial fathers hasn't changed much in the last decade. About 10% of all children of divorce live with a divorced father and stepmother, but only about 2% live *only* with their divorced father. This is in contrast to the 17% who live in one-parent homes in which there is only a mother.

Since they usually have more financial freedom, men are usually able to provide more physical comforts for their children, and they certainly are as equipped as women to provide nurturance, love, and acceptance. The decision of which parent should have custody should be based on which parent has the most flexibility in his or her lifestyle to juggle career and children. The percentage of fathers who are awarded custody will probably increase in the future, as women accept a man's ability to parent.

How Do You Handle New Love Interests?

Whichever parent has custody, there inevitably arises the question of new romantic interests, and how to handle them while being a single parent. Parents can begin new lives for themselves, they can move to new homes, and they can generally have new beginnings, but there is one thing they can't do, and that's to start all over again as virgins.

For sexually experienced, mature people, sexual intimacy with a person who is respected and liked is an important need. It doesn't stop being a need when parents are divorced, but attaining it without further traumatizing their children requires as much balance and patience as riding a unicycle on a tightwire over Niagra Falls.

For most mature adults—even those who go through a one-night-stand stage after divorce—sexual intimacy is most satisfying and most desirable when it is exclusively with one significant person. Sexual intimacy is thus a part of a general context of affection, companionship, and emotional support. One of the most striking differences between very young adults and more mature adults is that the young usually fall in love first and then become sexually intimate, while older adults are more likely to become sexually intimate first and then perhaps fall in love.

So the problem of being a divorced custodial parent is compounded by the mature, adult need for companionship, affection, emotional support, and sexual intimacy. Since divorcees have experienced the pain and destruction of marrying in love and divorcing in pain, many are reluctant to make another marital commitment without a good bit of time and contemplative thought. Furthermore, many divorced people are acutely aware that "love" is sometimes an ephemeral thing that may go as suddenly and as completely as it came, and they don't trust themselves any more to make promises to love somebody forever.

So what's a divorced parent to do in this kind of predicament? Do you let your lover move in? Do you let him just sleep over occasionally? Do you keep your romantic trysts strictly away from your home and always meet at his? And what if he has children at his house, too? Do you confine your lovemaking to motel rooms? Do you anachronistically "make out" on the living room sofa like teenagers and then send him home? Do you go ahead and get married in spite of your fears and hope it will work out?

The answer to these questions depends on the age of your child, on the length of time you've been divorced, and on the particular social climate in which you live. If your child is under the age of two and the lover in your life is familiar to him, your child will probably accept your friend at breakfast without any distress, especially if the man is warm and loving to him.

If he is over two and under six, however, and you've only recently been divorced, and the lover is not well known to your child, you'd best keep your sleeping arrangements discreet and early ended. Children of this age usually resent and are suspicious of somebody who isn't a family member turning up at the breakfast table or being in bed with Mommy in the morning. If your friend is not willing to go home at two in the morning in the interest of your child's emotional equilibrium, you've learned something about his maturity, and answered one of the questions regarding a future with him.

After the age of six, children usually know when somebody's in the bed with Mommy, even if they don't see him, and it makes them anxious and resentful. They're not sure what's happening, but they know they don't like it. They are vaguely resentful as if their mother was being disloyal to their father, and they are apt to show some behavioral problems as a sign of their displeasure.

If a lover moves in, children are quite likely to feel confused and resentful. Boys may begin to compete with the man for the position of importance with their mothers. Girls, on the other hand, may begin to compete with their mothers, and become precociously seductive toward the man. In some unconscious wish to punish their mothers for allowing a man other than their father to invade their homes and privacy, they may mimic their mothers in touching and caressing the man, and create a good bit of discomfort for both their mothers and the lover. In some cases, if the lover is particularly immature, a quasi-incestuous relationship may develop, much to the child's harm. In any case, the situation is one which can be hampering to a child's normal social and sexual development.

All these negative comments regarding a parent's sexual relationship after divorce may seem as if I'm espousing a Victorian sexual code. The fact is that I believe your sexual code should be your own business. If you believe that sex should be reserved for marriage, it would be a mistake for you to go against your own code of ethics and engage in premarital sex. On the other hand, if your sexual code is that responsible sexual intimacy is permissible—or desirable—with someone for whom you have affection and respect, then you should follow your own code.

The key word is "responsible." Part of responsible sexual conduct is consideration for one's partner and the partner's reputation, prevention of unwanted pregnancy, and keeping your sexual activities discreet and private so that others are not affected by them in any way. It's impossible to be an unmarried parent with a sleep-over lover and still be discreet or private, unless your children are away from home for the night. Since your home belongs to the family, and not just to you, such an arrangement is an invasion of your children's privacy, and not just of your bedroom.

So, while it may be inconvenient or frustrating, your child's best interests will be served if you keep your sexual activities away from home, especially if he is over the age of two years. To be sure, there are more cases every day in which two people have a monogamous, committed relationship which for all practical purposes is a marriage. They may choose, however, for various personal reasons, to remain legally single. In these instances, if the relationship is a long-standing one after several years of divorce and the child is old enough to share in the decision of all living together as a family, the relationship need not be damaging in any way.

The Illinois Supreme Court recently ruled that such a living arrangement constituted grounds for loss of custody, in an apparent attempt to reaffirm state laws against "fornication" and to uphold the concept of family. The Court notwithstanding, there are many things far more stressful to children than living with a divorced parent and another person in a family-like situation. The timing and the nature of the relationship is far more important to children than its legality.

It is especially unsettling to children for their parents to become romantically involved with a new person shortly after a divorce. Children need time to absorb a divorce before they can adjust to a new significant adult in their lifes. Generally speaking, in fact, children need at least a year to absorb their parents' divorce. They also need time to adjust to other significant changes, whether it is a major move, a change in schools, or some other important event. Since divorce frequently involves all these changes at one time, it is particularly important for a child to have time to gradually recover from their impact before a new change is introduced. It's not unusual for a school-aged child to take as much as two years following a divorce to fully recover his former emotional equilibrium.

Children usually don't object to parents dating different people after a divorce. In fact, they may become excited and help you dress, with embarrassing stage whispers when your date arrives of, "He's nice, why don't we marry him?" They don't even mind too much if you go away for the weekend, so long as you leave them with people they like and tell them all the exciting things you did when you get back.

But they do object to a sudden, strong shift in your loyalties, or a sudden all-absorbing focus of your attention to somebody else when they need it so much themselves. In this, as in all other areas, you simply have to be more grown up than your children are, and find a way to meet your own mature sexual needs without creating problems for your children.

You And Your Kids Are Still A Family

If you are divorced and without a romantic involvement, don't make the mistake of sitting around in bored dullness while you wait for one. You'll be teaching your child that you only exist when there is romance in your life. Get busy and do something you've always wanted to do. Learn something you never knew before. Volunteer some time to a community project you believe in. Go roller-skating or ice skating with your child. Go with him to the park and throw frisbies in the sunshine. Buy some foreign language records and learn with your child how to ask for a glass of water in three languages.

Don't, for heaven's sake, get into the habit of living with your child as if you're on a camping trip. Don't give him a plate of food and then retire to the living room and the telephone while he eats alone. Make mealtimes pleasant for both of you. Light candles, serve him apple juice in a wine glass to match your own, and play soft music. Enjoy pleasant conversation with him. You don't have to stop being civilized just because you're divorced!

Continue your life much as you would have done if you had stayed married, doing the same things you like to do, such as visiting art museums, the zoo, going to the theater, movies, church, PTA meetings, and having friends in to dinner or joining them in activities. Your child will learn by the way you live that life goes on and that happiness is something you create for yourself, and not something that rides on the shoulders of another person. By giving him an example of how you take the responsibility for your own happiness in life, you will give him a valuable lesson.

When he's older, your child will undoubtedly experience disappointments, broken love affairs, the loss of loved ones, and other painful situations. With a firm foundation in how to handle difficult times, he will be much better equipped to cry a lot, dust himself off, and go on living secure in the knowledge that life will hold something better for him just around the corner.

Learning to rebuild a life alone after a divorce may also be a positive learning experience for you. If you've never been alone or if you've never been forced to use your own resources in times of trouble, you may be pleasantly surprised to discover hidden strength and unexpected depth in yourself. If you allow your divorce and its aftermath to be a learning experience, you will bring to your next relationship more character and more of an expanded personality, which will add to its success.

You may remarry, or you may choose to remain unmarried. Whichever you choose, your life can certainly be a satisfying one, and your parenting ability and satisfaction can continue unabated. If you wish to remarry, your experience in finding happiness as a single parent will prevent your entering marriage simply out of boredom or insecurity. If you create a climate of serenity and self-confidence for yourself and your child, you will marry the next time–if you choose to marry–because marriage will add to the happiness you already have, and not because you want marriage to take away unmarried unhappiness. If you decide to remarry, you may be *happier*, but only if you have made youself happy while you were unmarried!